Document St

for Airlines and Other Aviation Businesses

by
LORI JO OSWALD, PH.D.

Wordsworth LLC

Publisher: Wordsworth LLC Publishing
PO Box 2397, Palmer, AK 99645
www.wordsworthwriting.net
To contact the author or publisher, e-mail: editor@wordsworthwriting.net

WORDSWORTH
Writing, Editing, & Document Formatting Svcs.

Words worth writing are ... words worth writing well.
Wordsworth ...
because your words are worth it.

TIPS FOR USING

Thank you for purchasing Wordsworth LLC's Style Guide for professional firms. This has been designed specifically for airlines and other aviation-related companies and their contractors but may be useful to other professional firms as well as individual writers.

This can be a useful training tool. The first six chapters can be assigned to personnel to read (it may take 2 to 3 hours); the rest can be used for reference on an as-needed basis.

If you would like to order a Microsoft Word version of this document to personalize it for your company, just order from our Web sites, either wordsworthwriting.net or formsinword.com. You may wish to substitute (or add to) your own acronym list, your own references style, your own font style, or your own sample documents. There are sections that are "rules" that should stay the same, and then there is a section titled Company Style, which can be changed.

I would like this to be a document that makes your job easier as well as makes the company look better, so your input is welcome and encouraged. If you have any questions or suggestions related to this style guide, I will be glad to answer them at no extra charge. Just e-mail your questions to us at editor@wordsworthwriting.net.

Our documents tell our clients a lot about us, and they should be error-free; it is therefore essential that you allow time for every document to be reviewed before it goes out. Thank you for caring about your company's words, style, and presentation!

Sincerely,
Lori Jo Oswald, Ph.D., Author
Owner, Wordsworth LLC

ACKNOWLEDGMENTS

I am grateful to the many technical editing clients I have worked with over the last 20 years.

For sources, I have used and highly recommend *Merriam-Webster's Collegiate Dictionary* and the *Chicago Manual of Style.* There are many other excellent references out there, but these are my two favorites.

Thank you to Eva Nagy, my assistant editor, for her suggestions on this document.

TABLE OF CONTENTS

LIST OF TABLES AND FIGURES

TABLES

FIGURES

1.0   INTRODUCTION

The purpose of this style guide is to provide writing tips, editing guidelines, and samples for your company. But this style guide has other functions as well. I have included specific acronym and style lists to help make report writing and editing at your company easier.

Consider this a guide in helping you through the writing or editing process. It is subject to change, and you are encouraged to add your suggestions and changes and give them to the technical editor for inclusion in future versions of this document.

Another element of this guide, and one which you might find slightly confusing, is that I have written it so that it not only guides you but also can *become* your own company style guide. (A Microsoft Word version can be purchased online at wordsworthwriting.net or formsinword.com if you wish to have it in Word for ease of adding your company's name and other personalizing touches.)

Why is a style guide important? The answers are consistency, clarity, and professionalism. Every document—e-mail, memo, letter, proposal, or report—gives an impression to clients or prospective clients about our company. As one editor said, "What we sell are reports." One mistake, such as writing 2.5 liters instead of .25 liters, can have serious consequences as well as make us seem unprofessional. Errors distract from messages, cause credibility problems, and can communicate the wrong information. Our clients expect and demand high-quality writing.

Do we expect you to catch every error or check for every possible item mentioned in this guide? Definitely not—this is mostly a reference manual and will mainly be used by the technical editor. There is no such thing as a perfect draft. The writer handles the prewriting and writing stages, while the technical editor edits and proofreads the document. Peer reviewers can also serve as helpful editors. This guide has sections for both writers and editors.

Editing and writing are different tasks and require different people to do them. All good writers have editors. When an editor makes changes, corrections, and suggestions on a copy, there is nothing personal intended toward the writer. This is simply a common—and important—

step in creating a strong, clear, and clean document.

Please don't let fear of your high school English teacher's red pen prevent you from passing on your company documentation to an editor. The editor does not judge you personally, talk about you, or think you are less of a person because your document has mistakes.

I will tell you an editor's secret: We love mistakes. We love finding and fixing them. We love thinking about words and the best ways they can be used to accomplish the assigned task. Additionally, a document with mistakes in it is much more interesting to read than a near-perfect one. And never once, in nearly 30 years of editing, have I thought poorly of an author because of the document I was reading. I think only of the words themselves, the purpose of the document as a whole, and the intended audience.

Most important is that the writer—and the company in general—knows that each document—no matter how small—should go through a review process, including the technical editor and at least one peer. Reviewers need to edit for the following:

- Grammar, punctuation, and spelling

- Style and format

- Organization and logical presentation

- Readability and appropriateness to the intended audience

- Inclusion of all required elements (i.e., Executive Summary, List of Acronyms and Abbreviations, References, etc.)

- Consistency and accuracy of data in the text, figures, and tables

- Figures, Tables, and References (text locations and consistent format)

There are many resources to help with writing and editing, in addition to this guide. An English handbook, such as those required in college English classes, is useful. I also rely on *Merriam-Webster's New Collegiate Dictionary* for final decisions about spelling, capitalization, and hyphenation. Another important source for editors, and for some of the information in this style guide, is the *Chicago Manual of Style*. It is an excellent, detailed manual that you should add to your library.

2.0 DOCUMENT REVIEW POLICY

As part of your company's commitment to quality control, all documents should go through the following review process (this may be different at your company):

- The initial document (or revision) is prepared by at least one employee, who then sends it to the technical editor.

- The author then submits the document to one or more qualified peers or supervisors. The reviewer keeps track changes on so that the author and technical editor can review those changes.

- The peer reviewer sends the document back to the author for revisions.

- The document is reviewed by a technical editor, who edits for grammar, content, organization, style, and formatting.

- The editor's changes are reviewed by the author. Track changes are accepted and comments are addressed and deleted, unless the author wants the peer reviewer to see them. Track changes for new sections or author changes are turned back on, so the editor can review these changes in the final version.

- The final version is e-mailed back to the technical editor who checks the changes by the author and peer reviewer and submits the document back to the author.

- The document is approved by a senior manager.

Since writing and editing are different processes requiring different skills, it is strongly recommended that all document writers obtain at least one edit from someone else.

Even formal letters and memos should be reviewed by someone other than the author. Proposals, letter reports, and draft and final reports should all be read—at a minimum—by a peer reviewer, a technical editor, and a senior reviewer.

Figure 2-1 shows the editing review process I recommend. Of course, not all companies can afford this complete process every time, but I hope if I convince you of nothing else in this manual, it is that a technical editor is an essential element in quality control. Your company will be presented to your clients as more professional, and you will reduce or eliminate risk in making embarrassing mistakes (often I have found inaccuracies in table or figure data and the text, for example).

All writers, including editors who write manuals, need an editor.

Figure 2-1   Document Review Flowchart

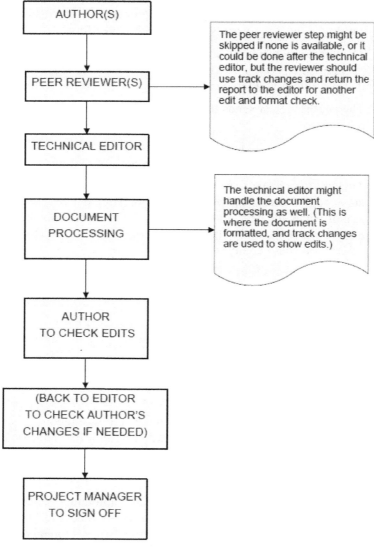

2.1   Peer Review

Peer and senior edits are made to evaluate the concepts and conclusions from a technical standpoint, as well as to provide any other feedback as needed. Remember, the more readers your document has before it goes to the client, the better!

2.2   Technical Editing

The technical editor, or someone else qualified to edit the report, should edit the document in the following areas:

- Evaluating grammar, punctuation, spelling, house style, and format (using this style guide as a source);

- Checking the organization of sections within the document, as well as the overall document;

- Looking for conciseness and readability;

- Making sure there is consistency among and within the text, tables, and figures;

- Determining whether there is a logical and clear progression from findings to conclusions; and

- Looking for the presence in the text of all the required sections.

Here are some specific areas the technical editor should check for in each document:

- Figures, graphs, and tables are clear;

- Data in text match data in tables, numbers in tables and figures are correct;

- Figures and tables are referred to in the text; figures and tables either directly follow the first textual reference, or are located on the next page following the first textual reference;

- An acronym (and abbreviation) list is included;

- Each acronym is defined the first time (and only the first time) it is used in the regular text (exceptions: Transmittal Letter, Executive Summary, figures and tables, and resumes are treated as separate documents);

- The use and capitalization of acronyms are correct (per the acronym list in this style guide);

- Font size and style are correct;

- References are in proper company format;

- Bullets are used instead of numbers with lists, unless numbers represent sequential steps;

- The use of *and/or* is avoided if possible;

- Appendices are referenced in order in the text and are complete;

- Maps are clear, legible, and checked for spelling;

- The text is not too technical-sounding or filled with jargon or vague phrases;

- Title page has proper elements, including the client's name and address, project number, and date;

- Table of Contents matches text, including page numbering, headings, appendices, and titles of tables and figures;

- Transmittal letter and executive summary are edited;

- The headings are worded properly to reflect the text that follows;

- There are enough headings; and

- The numbering and font styles of the headings are appropriate.

It is also important that the technical editor, the original writer, or a peer check the document after it is returned from document processing to be sure all changes were made correctly and that the formatting is still correct.

Try to understand the time needed by the technical editor to do a thorough edit. Although many reports require little editing (rewriting) but instead require mostly proofreading (fixing errors in grammar, punctuation, and style), the average time involved in technical editing is six pages per hour, which means a medium-length report will require at least 6 to 12 hours to complete. Figures and tables often add more time. Also, remember that the editor probably has other documents to complete before yours. Try not to say, "Just do a quick edit," to the editor. There is no good way to do that. You would be asking for a shoddy, incomplete job.

2.3   Document Processing (or Formatting)

The document processor puts the document in the proper format (i.e., report, proposal, letter, memo) using the appropriate fonts, margins, headings, footings, etc., according to the specifications in this style guide, unless other specifications are given by the author or technical editor.

The document processor also does the following:

- Adds the Table of Contents page
- Inserts tables and figures and the correctly formatted table and figure headings (using the "Captions" feature in Microsoft Word)
- Inserts page breaks
- Inserts page numbers

Nowadays, the technical editor often performs the Document Processing duties since documents are usually edited in Microsoft Word, on a computer. Some editors still prefer to mark up the hard copy; this can allow for a more careful, if slower, read, and if the company affords it and the editor prefers it, wonderful! Most of my clients are rushed, especially regarding proposals, and I am expected to do it all and quickly.

3.0   PUNCTUATION ("THE RULES")

This section lists common punctuation rules and errors with examples similar to the ones we encounter in your company's documents.

3.1   Apostrophes

- Apostrophes are not used for plural forms of years and acronyms: 1990s, USTs.

- Apostrophes are used to show possession. The apostrophe precedes the "s" when the noun is singular; it follows the "s" when the noun is plural. There is no need for a second "s" after the apostrophe. Examples: the client's bill, the USEPA's decision, Robert Edwards' letter, your company's documents.

- Its and it's are often confused; *its* is the possessive form, and *it's* is a contraction for *it is*. Examples: The agency believed its decision was correct. It's not important to me. (Do not use it's in technical writing; see next bullet item.)

- Do not use contractions: it's, can't, don't, won't, wouldn't, etc.

3.2   Capitalization

- Generally, we tend to use capitals unnecessarily. If you are not sure, you probably do not need to capitalize the word. To be sure, you can use *Merriam-Webster's New Collegiate Dictionary*; if it is capitalized there, go ahead and capitalize it. Also, follow the guidelines in this section.

- Acronyms and abbreviations are usually in all capital letters, although the words they are based on are often not capitalized. To be sure, check the abbreviations and acronyms list in Section 13.0 of this style guide. Example: inside diameter variation (IDV).

- Capitalize titles only when they directly precede a person's name or are part of an address: The source of the information was Project Manager Jane Szmanski. The project manager is Jane Szmanski. Jane Szmanski, project manager, is. . . .

- Generally, capitalize counties, states, municipalities, cities, and boroughs when they are part of a name. They are usually lowercased when they precede a name: Kansas City, the Municipality of Anchorage, the state of Alaska, the city of Palmer, Washington State, the Pacific Northwest (the proper name of a region), northern Washington (a general direction).

- If you are referring to a specific document, table, entity, or organization, capitalize it. If not, lowercase: draft reports, *Draft Report 1 for Bethel Landfill*, Figure 1-5; the figure; the Environmental Services Agency; the agency; the Federal Bureau of Standards; federal, state, municipal, and city agencies; the federal Department of Transportation; the federal government; Congress and the Senate; the state senate and the state legislature; the department; the Department of Public Works.

- Do not capitalize "the" before a company or institution name: the University of Alaska Anchorage.

- Capitalize the first word in columns and bullet lists if each item is a complete sentence or is particularly lengthy. For simple words or short phrases that finish the sentence preceding the bullet list, lowercase the individual bullet items, use commas or semicolons at the end of each item as is appropriate, and end the final list item with a period. For example:

    The ground is

    - hard,

    - cold, and

    - dark.

- Capitalize specific geographic names but not general terms: John, Paul, and Mary creeks, Yukon River, the lakes, Lake Ontario, lakes Stephan and Willamette, Winston Lake.

3.3   Colons

- Colons are often used to precede lists. They are also used to precede clauses or phrases that clarify or illustrate.

- Use only one space after a colon (and after a semicolon, for that matter). The contractor discovered three flaws: first, a loose bolt; second, a missing nut; and third, a broken screw.

- Colons in text are used after complete sentences (i.e., you should be able to replace the colon with a period). The same rule should apply to colons before bullet lists (but we are flexible here and allow for an incomplete sentence before a bullet list if necessary). Examples: We have six requests: the first . . . , the second . . . , etc. Bring four items to the campsite: food, bedding, equipment, and bear spray.

- In the text, do not use a colon after the word "includes" or "including" unless the words "the following" appear after. Example: The punctuation list includes commas, semicolons, and periods. The list includes the following: cheese, bread, and water. It is acceptable to use a colon after "includes" or "including" before a bullet list, but it is still preferable to have a complete sentence before any colon.

- Although you usually need a complete sentence before a colon, you do not need one after a colon. However, it is not wrong to have a complete sentence after a colon. Examples: I have six pets: two dogs, two cats, and two horses. The monitoring well data were incomplete: additional testing was required. (Note: The writer could have used a semicolon, a period, or a comma with a conjunction [and] instead of a colon in the last sentence.)

- Use a colon after a salutation in a letter instead of a comma (Dear Mr. Jones:).

- A colon can be used after one word, as we have been using throughout this document with the word "Example." Example: This is such a case. For example: Here is another one.

- When the expressions namely, for instance, for example, or that is are used in a sentence to introduce a list, a comma is usually used instead of a colon. Example: Birch's study included the three most critical areas, namely, McBurney Point, Rockland, and Effingham.

3.4   Commas

Comma rules can be confusing, so we have provided subheadings for each use to help you find the appropriate rule quickly.

3.4.1   Using Commas in a Series

Always use a comma before "and" or "or" in a series of three or more items. This is a style requirement, not a rule. You might notice that most newspapers use Associated Press (AP) style, which does not use the last comma in a series. Most magazines use the *Chicago Manual of Style*, which does require it. It is standard in formal writing to use the comma. For example:

- Mammals in Area A include caribou, fox, and lemmings; mammals in Area B include polar bear, walrus, and several species of whales and seals.

- It was a fast, simple, and inexpensive process.

Incorrect in Technical Writing: The corporation requires its employees to be loyal, hard working and prepared.

Correction: The corporation requires its employees to be loyal, hard working, and prepared.

When adjectives modifying the same noun can be reversed and make sense, or when they can be separated by either "and" or "or," they should be separated by commas:

- The drawing was of a modern, sleek, swept-wing airplane.

But when an adjective modifies a phrase, no comma is needed, as in the following example, where *damaged* modifies *radar beacon system*.

- The company investigated the damaged radar beacon system.

If there are only two items in a series, no comma is necessary.

- The drawing was of a modern sleek airplane.

3.4.2   Using Commas to Separate Complete Sentences

If you have two independent clauses (i.e., complete sentences that could stand on their own) separated by a coordinating conjunction (and, but, for, or, so, yet), put a comma before the coordinating conjunction. If the second clause is not an independent clause, do not use the comma before the coordinating conjunction.

- The pack ice breaks off from shore ice in June, and the shore is free of ice from late July until mid-August.

- The Gubik formation is mainly of marine origin and consists of lenses of gravel, sand, silt, and clay.

3.4.3 Using Commas to Set off Phrases (Which, That, Who)

Usually, when you use the relative pronoun "which," you have a phrase that needs to be set off from the rest of the sentence with two commas. Usually when "that" is used, there are no commas. Whether or not to use commas before and after a clause beginning with "who" depends on the meaning of the sentence. If the information following the word "who" is essential to the meaning of the sentence, do not use commas; if it can be eliminated without changing the meaning of the sentence, do use commas.

- The company's new style guide, which will be in use by December 1, ensures consistency in all documents.

- The style guide that the company is presently using is outdated.

- The editor, who studied at the University of Washington, is based in the Fresno office.

- The editor who is the most skilled in that area is in the Palmer office.

3.4.4 Using Commas with Names, Titles, and Addresses

Commas are used to separate distinct items in the text. Therefore, if you write an address on one line, separate the elements in this way: Chris Polsky, 4117 Ravensdale Road, Seattle, Washington. Note that the state is spelled out in the text, but in letters and addresses, use the postal code abbreviation (listed in Section 13.0, Abbreviations and Acronyms):

Chris Polsky
4117 Ravensdale Road
Seattle, WA 97506
(206) 777-7677

Dear Chris Polsky:

Note that in the salutation, above, a colon is used instead of a comma in formal writing. Also, I addressed "Chris Polsky" instead of "Mr." or "Ms." Polsky because I am not sure whether Chris is a man or a woman, based on the name.

Here are some additional uses of commas with names, titles, and addresses:

- Toronto, Ontario, Canada

- Sally Jo Rogers, Ph.D.

- John Smith, P.E.

- LMB, Inc.

3.4.5 Using Commas in Numbers

Use a comma in numbers larger than 999: 131,000, 9,000, 800.

3.4.6 Using Commas after Introductory Phrases

In technical writing, always use a comma after an introductory phrase, in order to avoid confusion. For example, notice how the comma clarifies this confusing sentence: To be successful managers with MBAs must continue to learn. <u>Revised</u>: To be successful, managers with MBAs must continue to learn.

3.4.7 Using Commas with Quotation Marks

Commas and periods always go inside the closing quotation marks; semicolons and colons always go outside closing quotation marks.

- Smith said, "I didn't do it," after he saw me.

- I said, "Yes, you did."

- I don't know why he said he "didn't"; it was clear that he did.

3.4.8 Using Commas in Dates

- August 27, 1999, was the day he proposed.

- The subcontractor conducted the site assessment in June 1998.

3.5 Dangling and Misplaced Modifiers

Dangling modifiers can be tricky to spot, but the rewards are worth it. A dangling modifier is a word or phrase that modifies a word which does not appear in the sentence (or is in the wrong part of a sentence). Here are some examples (the first two are from grammar.about.com):

- Sipping cocktails on the balcony, the moon looked magnificent. (This sounds like the moon drinks.)

- Exhausted after the long hike, the shady hammock was a welcome sight. (How can a hammock be exhausted?)

- After looking behind the garbage container, the polar bear was located.

Spotting these can be challenging, but fixing them is easy. Add in the subject. For the third bullet item above, for example, add the missing subject after the comma: After looking behind the garbage container, the scientist found the polar bear.

Here are some more humorous examples from eddiesnipes.com:

- While reading the newspaper, the cat jumped on the table.

- The young girl was walking the dog in a short skirt.

- The dog was chasing the boy with the spiked collar.

- The hunter crouched behind a tree waiting for a bear to come along with a bow and arrow.

- The woman walked the dog in purple suede cowboy boots.

- We saw dinosaurs on a field trip to the natural history museum.

- Hopping briskly through the vegetable garden, I saw a toad.

3.6   Dashes

Dashes come in three lengths: hyphens (-) (which are discussed in Section 3.9), en dashes (–), and em dashes (—).

3.6.1   En Dashes

- Our company's style is generally to have one space around en dashes. En dashes are the shorter dash.

- Microsoft Word will automatically change a hyphen to an en dash as you type, as long as you have the space before and after the hyphen.

3.6.2   *Em Dashes*

- Dashes are usually used to emphasize the text in between them—to tell the reader this is important and look here—so they should be used sparingly.

- Dashes can also be used to define words. Anorexia nervosa—an eating disorder characterized by an aversion to eating and an obsession with losing weight—is common among young female gymnasts and ballet dancers.

- Type two hyphens with no spaces around them, and Microsoft Word should automatically replace them with a dash.

- There are no spaces around em dashes.

3.7   Ellipses

Ellipsis points (plural: ellipses) are a set of three or four spaced dots (periods on the keyboard) showing missing text from quotations. Usually you can quote without having to resort to using them (as in the first example below), but here are some ways they are used.

- Example without ellipsis: Peter Singer said that stones "do not have interests" because they can't suffer, while a mouse does have "an interest in not being kicked down the road, because it will suffer if it is" (1975).

- Quotation with ellipsis: Yi-Fu Taun, author *of Dominance and Affection: The Making of Pets*, said that the breeding process is used to make animals more useful or desirable for humans: "With the horse . . . humans have tried to make the animal both larger and smaller" (1984).

- Use a fourth "dot"—a sentence-ending period—along with the ellipsis points when an ellipsis comes at the end of your sentence or when the material you have deleted contains at least one period: Summer also said that people have described personal space as "a small shell, a soap bubble, an aura. . . ." In *Animal Liberation*, Peter Singer wrote, "Nearly all the external signs which lead us to infer pain in other humans can be seen in other species. . . . Behavioral signs—writhing, facial contortions, moaning, yelping or other forms of calling, attempts to avoid the source of pain, appearance of fear at the prospect of its repetition, and so on—are present" (1975).

- Note spacing requirements: with three "dots," space before and after each one; with four dots, do not space before the first one (or after the last one if a quotation mark immediately follows it).

- The ellipsis points should not be separated at the end of a line and into the following line. This can be a problem in right-justified text. You may have to revise your sentence to fix it.

3.8 Exclamation Points

- Avoid! Avoid! Avoid! They do not belong in formal writing! In fact, most good writers don't use them at all, except perhaps in a quotation! (Jane screamed, "Eeek!") And especially never use more than one!! That would be most inappropriate!!!!!!!

3.9 Hyphenation

- Hyphens connect related items, often modifiers that precede a noun (tie-in, toll-free call, two-thirds, one-year-old child).

- Hyphens are often used unnecessarily after prefixes. Check the lists in *Merriam-Webster's New Collegiate Dictionary* if in doubt. (To save time, nowadays I go to www.m-w.com and just type in the words I need to check there.)

- Here are some examples of words that do *not* take hyphens after the prefixes: preexisting, semivolatile, nonprofit, nonhazardous, nonnegotiable. See Table 3-1 for a list of prefixes that do not usually take a hyphen (always confirm at www.m-w.com or in your Merriam-Webster's dictionary if you can).

- For the examples in which *Chicago Manual of Style* does not take a hyphen but Merriam-Webster's does (e.g., coworker or co-worker and prolife or pro-life), I usually go with Merriam-Webster's dictionary. It is my "go-to" source for capitalization, hyphens, and spelling. I have included, in this manual, a list of commonly used (and confused) words; I use them exactly as in that list.

Table 3-1   Prefixes Not Requiring Hyphens

Prefix	Example	Exception
after	aftereffect	
anti	antisocial	
bi	bilingual	

Prefix	Example	Exception
co	coworker	*Note: Merriam-Webster's does use a hyphen with most co- words.*
counter	counterbalance	
equi	equilibrium	
extra	extracurricular	
infra	infrared	
inter	interstimulus	
intra	intraspecific	
macro	macrocosm	
mega	megawatt	
meta	metacognitive	meta-analysis
micro	microorganism	
mid	midterm	
mini	minisession	
multi	multiphase	
non	nonsignificant	non-achievement-oriented students
over	overaggressive	
post	posttest	*I know it looks like "post" should take a hyphen, but check the list in Webster's (or m-w.com); it rarely does. Still, if a company insists or its style guide demands, I will not argue, and I will use the hyphen.*
pre	preexperimental	pre-1970, pre-UAA trial
pro	prowar	*Note: Merriam-Webster's does use hyphens with most "pro-" words.*
pseudo	pseudoscience	
re	reevaluate	re-pair (pair again), re-form (form again)
semi	semidarkness	
socio	socioeconomic	
sub	subtest	
super	superordinate	
supra	supraliminal	
ultra	ultrahigh	
un	unbiased	un-ionized (not ionized)
under	underdeveloped	

Source: *Chicago Manual of Style*

- Exceptions to the above include the following: if the prefix stands alone (pre- and postclosure elements), if the root word is capitalized (mid-August, non-American), if the root is a number (pre-1900), if the resulting word can have two meanings (retreat and re-treat or un-ionized and unionized), or if the second element consists of more than one word (non-English-speaking, non-achievement-oriented students).

- Generally, hyphenate words with the prefixes ex, all, and self and the suffix elect: all-encompassing, self-employed, president-elect.

- Hyphenate a numeral and a unit of measure used as an adjective: three 1,000-gallon tanks; 3-, 4-, and 6-inch-diameter pipes.

- Do not use a hyphen after adverbs ending in –ly: previously installed wells.

- Do not hyphenate Latin terms: in situ (per Webster's; you will see this term handled differently by different companies and agencies however, so if a client prefers another way—hyphenated or italicized or both—go ahead and use that style for that client.

- Hyphenate two words of equal value used as modifiers: gray-brown soil.

- Hyphenate compound modifiers when one word modifies or defines another but does not separately define the noun being referred to: dark-green building (but no hyphen in large green building, since large does not modify green).

- Before a noun, hyphenate a compound consisting of a noun and a participle: decision-making skills, broad-based experience. But do not hyphenate if the expression follows the noun: Her experience is broad based. The well is 73 feet deep.

- Hyphenate a phrase used as an adjective before a noun (up-to-date account) but not if it follows the noun (the account was up to date).

- Hyphenate compounds containing numbers that precede the noun: 23-year-old woman, twentieth-century innovation, one-year program, 7-foot depth, 7-foot-wide opening. But there is no hyphen in the following: in three years, 35 gallons of fuel, the woman was 23 years old.

- Hyphenate fractions that are spelled out: one-half, two-thirds.

- Hyphenate when referring to specific figures and tables: Figure 4-1, Table 3-7.

- Although most of the time numerals 10 and over are not spelled out, if you must begin a sentence with a compound number, do spell out and use a hyphen: forty-six, one hundred sixty-three.

3.10   Parentheses and Brackets

Generally, try not to overuse parentheses. Some editors believe that if it is not important enough to include as part of the text, then delete it. If it is important, set it off with commas or dashes instead. But, of course, sometimes it is necessary or useful to include parenthetical expressions. So here are some tips to guide you:

- Periods go inside parentheses when a complete sentence is contained within the parentheses. (We have tentatively scheduled this meeting for June 16, 2001.) Otherwise, put the period outside the parentheses: Previous studies found the landfill area safe (Compton, 1989).

- No other punctuation mark should directly precede the first parenthesis mark. The findings were explained by Smith (1989), and they were confirmed by Jones (1993).

- Within a parenthetical phrase, if you have another parenthetical phase, use brackets: Buck (in *The Call of the Wild* [1903] by Jack London) was one of the most developed dog characters in literature.

- However, for code regulations that already contain parentheses, use brackets on the outside where you would normally use parentheses: [24 CFR 1600(4)(5)].

3.11   Quotation Marks

- Quotation marks are used only around direct quotes (i.e., words taken from a source exactly as they were written). If you are changing or condensing the information from another source, still give credit, but do not use quotation marks. The latter is an indirect quote.

- — Direct Quote, Complete Sentence: John Smith said, "This is wrong."

- — Direct Quote, Word or Phrase Only: Darrell Cohen said he is "positive" the actions were appropriate.

- — Direct Quote, Word or Phrases with Material Deleted: According to Daniel Danielson, the site was "always empty . . . and left alone."

- — Direct Quote, Complete Except Material Deleted from End of Sentence: Patricia Meyers said, "I don't think I can agree with that assessment. . . ."

- — Direct Quote, Material Missing from Beginning of Quoted Sentence: Hillary Capra said that the area "is in need of a bulldozer and explosives." (Note: There are no ellipses marks used at the beginning of a partial quotation; the word "that" preceding the quote as well as the lower case "is" tell the reader that this is not a complete quotation.)

- — Indirect Quote: John Smith said that he disagrees with Mark Benson on the results.

- Periods and commas always go inside quotation marks: John Smith said, "I don't think so," and Jane Doe said, "I agree."

- Colons and semicolons always go outside quotation marks: John Smith said he is firmly "committed"; his partner is undecided.

- Single quotation marks are used only within double quotation marks: John Smith said, "James told me, 'I am sure,' before he left."

- When quotations are longer than four lines or 40 words, remove the quotation marks, introduce the quotation, and set the direct quotation off with two indents, as in the following example (for readability, we have indented this example more than 10 spaces or 2 tabs, so that you can see the indent easier in this bulleted section). In *Handbook of Technical Writing*, Alread, Brusaw, and Oliu (2000) explained how to set off quotations:

> Material that is four lines or longer (MLA) or at least 40 words (APA) is usually inset; that is, it is set off from the

body of the text by being indented from the left margin ten spaces (MLA) or five to seven spaces (APA). The quoted passage is spaced the same as the surrounding text and is not enclosed in quotation marks. . . . If you are not following a specific style manual, you may block indent 10 spaces from both the right and left margins for reports and other documents.

3.12   Semicolons

Everyone should have a favorite punctuation mark, in my view. Mine is the semicolon. But semicolons are only used in two ways.

- The first and the most common is between two independent clauses not joined by a conjunction (examples of conjunctions include *and, or, for, so, but, yet*): I am right; you are wrong.

  Often, these sentences contain a transition word or phrase such as *however, furthermore, for example, consequently*, or *moreover*. The semicolon precedes the transitional word or phrase as long as there is a complete sentence both before and after it: I believe I am right; however, I am open to suggestions. I do not, however, agree. (Note that there is a comma after the transitional word when a semicolon precedes it.)

- The second use of the semicolon is to clarify a list that contains commas. The semicolon separates elements that go together. For example: I have lived in Anchorage, Alaska; Eugene, Oregon; New York, New York; and Seattle, Washington.

4.0 COMPANY STYLE

This section lists our "house style" for document text issues. Many of these items are not necessarily "rules" of grammar or punctuation. Instead, the word "style" refers to a company's preferences for how such items as acronyms, commas in a series, capitalization, justification, and italics are used.

There are almost as many styles as there are companies and publications. Newspapers, for example, usually use the Associated Press (AP) style. The styles I have chosen for this style guide is based on standards in the technical writing industry, the *Chicago Manual of Style,* and the Government Printing Office style, as well as the preferences of our clients. These are subject to change. However, it is important to be consistent within documents themselves, and within our company. Therefore, try to follow these style guidelines when writing your document. The technical editor will also look to make sure that all documents meet our style requirements; therefore, do not worry if you are not sure of something or do not have time to check everything. This is the editor's job, and this section is mainly written for editors and document processors to use. This is probably the most important section of this style guide, as it sets down the guidelines for our own company's style.

4.1 Abbreviations and Acronyms

- There is no need to use an abbreviation if a term is only used once. Just spell out the term. (Example: The U.S. Environmental Protection Agency is . . .)

- If using an abbreviation more than once, place it in parentheses after the complete term first appears. From then on, use the abbreviation only. (Example: The U.S. Environmental Protection Agency (USEPA) is . . . According to the USEPA . . .)

- Generally, do not use "the" before abbreviations (example: TPH was detected). Exceptions are certain government agencies (the USEPA, the ADEC).

- Abbreviations and acronyms are generally treated as singular nouns (the USEPA is the agency overseeing the program). Make acronyms plural by adding s (no apostrophe), as in VOCs. Only use the apostrophe for possession (the FDA's position).

- TPH and BTEX are collective nouns that take singular verbs; do not add the "s" to them: Total petroleum hydrocarbons were detected; TPH was detected.

- Do not define U.S., Latin abbreviations (etc.), or compass directions (NE). Some companies prefer not to define F (for Fahrenheit) or C (for Celsius) as well. Abbreviations do not contain periods, except U.S., in., Mr., Ms., no. (number), p. (page), pp. (pages), Latin abbreviations (i.e., et al., etc., e.g.), and degrees (Ph.D., M.A., B.S.).

- Some companies and agencies capitalize all words in their acronyms list, but I do not. I follow the correct capitalization for that term. For example, I capitalize Quality Assurance Plan (QAP) when it is referring to a specific company plan but not when it is referring to such plans in general (QAP is all caps in either case, of course).

- The original words that the acronym represents are not necessarily capitalized; see the abbreviations and acronyms list in Section 13.0 of this document to be sure. (Example: method reporting limit [MRL]).

- Articles agree with the pronunciation of the acronym: an MSDS (em ess dee ess), a RCRA assessment (rik-rah).

- Latin (i.e., e.g., etc.). You do not need to define Latin abbreviations. But do make sure you are using them correctly. i.e. means that is, e.g. means for example, and etc. means and so forth or and so on. Check Merriam-Webster's Tenth New Collegiate Dictionary if you are not sure of the meaning of a Latin abbreviation (see the abbreviations section near the back of the dictionary).

- Always use a comma after i.e. and e.g. Also, they should be used in parenthetical text only: The tanks hold two liquids (i.e., gasoline and methanol).

- If etc. ends a sentence, do not add a second period. Usually you can avoid using etc. by revising the text to include a phrase such as "and others" or "and so on." Another way is to revise the phrase that precedes a list by adding the word includes or including. Instead of writing *The mammals I saw were moose, elk, rabbits, etc.* write *The mammals I saw included moose, elk, and rabbits.*

- Treat résumés, executive summaries, transmittal letters, and figures and tables as separate documents. Redefine acronyms and abbreviations in them. Provide a key to all acronyms and abbreviations used in the tables and figures; the key goes at the bottom of the table or figure.

Section 13.0 contains lists of commonly used acronyms and abbreviations in this field. However, you may find that some have changed or that your company has others to add to this list. If searching on the Internet for the correct spelling, capitalization, and usage of an acronym or abbreviation, I prefer to find government agency Web sites for sources. You will find many errors online, of course, and it may take some searching to find a reliable source. By including the acronyms and abbreviations sections in this document, I hope to have saved you time.

4.2   Companies and Agencies

- Use the name as the company or agency does on its official documents. It may contain and, &, Inc., Co., or Company.

- You can shorten Company to Co. and Incorporated to Inc.

- Usually there is a comma before "Inc.," but if the company is not using a comma in its official documents, leave it out.

- A company is singular, so it takes a singular verb. Also, if you use a pronoun to reference the company, use "it" instead of "they."

  Example: Champion Word Services is skilled in providing detailed editing to corporate documents. It is also . . .

  Since the word "it" is a bit awkward sounding, this is a good place to use an acronym [CWS] as long as it is defined previously; to use "The company"; to use the company's full name again; or to combine the two sentences and eliminate the need for the subject to be repeated (e.g., Champion Word Services is skilled in providing detailed editing of corporate documents and in providing quality workshops to corporate personnel).

4.3   Company, Software, and Equipment Names

As a technical editor, you will find it useful to keep lists of items you use frequently in documents, including the following:

- acronyms and abbreviations;

- previous projects (with exact titles);

- company names (including subcontractors that you might use in proposals, for example);

- software titles; and

- equipment (again, you might list these in proposals).

Although I have included an acronyms list at the end of this document, company names are so numerous and varied that it will be necessary to create your own.

I often see inconsistency in company and product names in documents, which is why I added this section. Specific inconsistencies are seen in capitalization, spelling, and spacing of equipment and software names. The purpose of this list is to provide an accurate, exact list of all of company, software, and equipment names; keep the list updated; and avoid confusion and inconsistencies in your documents.

Below, I have provided some examples from company, software, and equipment based on hydrographic surveying, for an example of what you might create for your own company.

4.3.1   Company Names Examples

The following company spellings, for example, including capitalization, spelling, hyphenation, were checked on company Web sites. Whenever possible, I included in my list the company Web site address for checking additional products, updating names, and other questions.

Triton Elics International (can use Triton or TEI for multiple uses; just define first use)

Products:

BathyPro™
Bathy+Plus™
DelphMap™
DelphNav™

Delph Seismic®+Plus

HydroSuite™

Isis® Sonar

SeaClass™

SGIS™

Thales GeoSolutions Group Ltd.

Thales Geosolutions (Pacific) Inc.

Trimble®

4.3.2 Equipment Names

These equipment names have been taken directly from company Web sites, so the spacing, spelling, capitalization, and the use of the TM or R symbols should be correct. Whenever possible, I have inserted the company (manufacturer's) name in parentheses after the equipment or software name. The rule on the ™ or ® symbol is to either use the symbol throughout the document or to use it at least the first time the product is mentioned in a document (the company would no doubt prefer the first technique, but for proposals, I usually use the second; for published reports, I use the first [i.e., list TM or R symbol with every mention]).

AutoCAD

AutoCAD/MAP

Bathy+Plus™ (Triton Elics International)

BathyPro™ (Triton Elics International)

CARIS®

CARIS® HIPS

CARIS® SIPS

Delph Seismic®+Plus (Triton Elics International)

DelphMap™ (Triton Elics International)

DelphNav™ (Triton Elics International)

Echotrac (use Odom Echotrac)

ESRI

HydroBat (Reson software)

HydroSuite™ (Triton Elics International)

HYPACK®

HYPACK® MAX

Isis® (side-scan sonar acquisition system made by Triton Elics International)

Isis® Sonar (Triton Elics International)

MapInfo

MicroStation (made by Bentley Systems Inc.)

Morad Electronics Corp. (manufacturer of antennas)

Odom

Odom Echotrac (a dual-frequency survey echo sounder)

ORE Offshore

ORE Offshore Trackpoint (Be specific: Trackpoint 4440A or Trackpoint II; give full name if possible)

Polaris Imaging

Polaris Imaging EOSCAN® (a sonar data acquisition and display system)

Reson (full name of U.S. company: Reson Inc.)

SeaBat (Reson software)

SeaClass™ (Triton Elics International)

Seapath 200 (made by Seatex Inc.)

SGIS™ (Triton Elics International)

Tripod Data Systems (a Trimble® company)

Triton Elics International (can use Triton or TEI for multiple uses; just define first use)

Triton Isis®

WaterLOG®

WinFrog (Thales Geosolutions)

4.4   Dates

- Do not add letters to a date: June 27, not June 27th.

- Do not shorten: 1970s, not '70s

- Use a comma with month, day, and year: August 18, 1999, was the date of the test.

- Do not abbreviate months in text (okay in figures and tables): December, not Dec.

- Only use an apostrophe with a date if it is possessive. Examples: The 1990s were very good years. In my experience, 1974's best song was "Me and Mrs. Jones."

4.5   Headings and Titles

- Capitalize the first word, the major parts of speech (nouns, adjectives, adverbs, and verbs), other parts of speech with four or more letters (including prepositions with four or more letters), and the last word in all levels of headings: Memory in Hearing-Impaired Children, On-Site Wells, Playing With Fire.

- Do not use 0.0, 0.1, 0.2, etc. as a chapter heading. The first chapter should begin with "1," as in 1.0, 1.1, 1.2, etc. The Transmittal Letter, the Abbreviations and Acronym List, and the Executive Summary do not have heading numbers.

- The following are the fonts normally used in standard company reports. You do not need to format the fonts; they are provided here for your information. The technical editor or document processer will take care of this. You also should never number your headings; this is automatically done by document processing using the styles feature in Microsoft Word.

  — Caps, Centered, bold, Arial 14, *number at left is 4.0*

  — All caps, left justified, bold, Arial 12, *number at left is 4.1*

  — Upper and lowercase, left, bold, Arial 11, *number at left is 4.1.1*

  — Upper and lowercase, number is indented .5 (1 tab), no bold, italic, Arial 10, *number at left is 4.1.1.1*

  — Fifth-level heading. Italics, Arial 10, underlined, *do not use number at left*

4.5.1   Heading Introductions

Always write at least a one-sentence introduction under a heading title before going on to another heading title. For example: This section describes the 2002 remediation activities at the Bethel Landfill.

4.6   Italics

- Generally, avoid italics in formal writing, except for the following examples.

  — Italicize the names of vessels: the *Exxon Valdez*.

— Italicize the taxonomic names of genera, species, and varieties: The mountain is covered by second-growth forests of Douglas fir (*Pseudotsuga menziesii*).

— Italicize foreign words and phrases only if they have not yet entered common usage (do not italicize in situ; this is commonly used).

— In the text and in the reference list, italicize titles of major documents; do not use quotation marks around such titles: *Final Report: Bethel Landfill Cleanup.* When you refer to chapters or articles within larger works (such as an article within a journal), use quotation marks around the shorter work's title: In "The Story of the Essay," from Jane Doe's *English Secrets,* we learn that every successful essay has a thesis. Do not put quotation marks around section titles of reports, however. Example: Section 1.0 of this document contains an overview of the work performed.

- Do not italicize punctuation that precedes or follows italicized words or sections.

- Do not italicize punctuation before or after an italicized word, just those that are part of the italicized material.

4.7 Justification

You have two choices with company style: left justification or full justification. Some believe that full justification looks more professional. Tests reveal that left justification (i.e., ragged right) is more readable, especially with lengthy and technical material. Therefore, it is acceptable to use ragged right in your company documents.

4.8 Lists (Bulleted and Numbered Lists)

Bullet styles vary from company to company and from style book to style book. These are guidelines for our company documents but are always subject to change. For now, these are our preferences.

- Generally, bullets are preferred to numbers for lists. Numbers can be used in sequential steps.

- Perhaps most important is the introductory sentence or phrase to the list. Again, there are lots of styles and discussions on this, but for consistency, the following outlines our company's preferred style. It is up to you, or to the editor, whether to use a colon after the last word preceding the bullet list even though the sentence might be a fragment (e.g., The three tests run were:). If you can make a complete sentence to precede the colon, this is preferred. One way to do this is to add the words "the following" to the clause you have and then use a colon. Example: The methods used will include the following:

- Note that if you use the word "include" or "including" in your introductory sentence, you have an incomplete list following. Drop the "include" if you have a complete list. The animals seen included wolves, moose, and ptarmigan. (Other animals were also seen.) The animals seen were wolves, moose, and ptarmigan. (No other animals were seen.)

- It is important that each bullet item be parallel to the others. Therefore, if one is a complete sentence with a period, the others should all be complete sentences with periods.

- If each bullet item is not a complete sentence, do not use periods. Also, make sure they each follow the introductory sentence (i.e., that they make sense when joined with the introductory sentence).

- If you use commas at the end of the bullet items, add the word "and" after the last comma (i.e., the second to last bullet item), and insert a period at the end of the last bullet item.

- If there are commas within bulleted items, but the entire bullet list is part of a complete sentence, use semicolons instead of commas at the end of each bullet item (and a period at the end).

- Capitalize the first word of each item in a list if each item is a complete sentence or is lengthy. Include the period as well in these cases. Do not capitalize the first word and use commas (or semicolons as described above) if the bullet items consist of one or a few words and merely complete the sentence introducing them. For example:

  Laboratory quality control (QC) samples will include:
  - method blanks,

- laboratory control sample duplicates, and
- matrix spike duplicate samples.

4.9   Measurements

- Use figures (i.e., don't spell out) for numbers that refer to measurements: 8 cm wide, 9 percent, 8 years old, 5-mg dose, 4 miles, 6 minutes, 3 inches, 7 acres.

- Spell out simple units in the text, such as inch, acre, liter, minute, and year. But if they are part of a complex unit, use the abbreviation (define first use just as you would with any abbreviation): ft/min, mg/L.

- Abbreviated measurements are written the same whether singular or plural. For example, lb can refer to both pound and pounds.

- Most measurement abbreviations do not take a period. Some do, however (in. for inch). See the list of measurement abbreviations in Section 13.0 to be sure.

4.10   Numbers

- Generally, spell out numbers less than 10 (one, three), and use numerals for 10 and higher (14, 256).

- Always use numerals to express measurement (2 feet, 4 mg/L, 7 gmp, 5 pore volumes), time (10 p.m.), parts of a document (Chapter 4, Phase 4, Section 2, Item 3, Table 6-1, Figure 2-3), money ($3 million), very large numbers followed by million or billion (7 million), percentages and decimal fractions (3 percent, 3.14, 1.2), and ratios (1 to 10).

- When two or more numbers are listed in a group in the same sentence, and one or more is 10 or more, use numerals for all:

    — The laboratory evaluated 7 of the 12 samples.

    — The contractor drilled 12 borings to a depth of 70 feet and completed 4 of the 12 borings as vapor extraction wells.

    — The contractor drilled six borings to a depth of 70 feet and completed four of the six borings as vapor extraction wells.

- Spell out all numbers that start a sentence: Twelve test holes were analyzed. You can also rewrite the sentence to move the number: *XYZ Company* analyzed 12 test holes.

- When numbers appear together in the same phrase, it is often a good practice to express one as a word and one as a number (XYZ *Company* purchased fourteen 8-inch pipes) but not in a list (XYZ *Company* purchased 6-, 8-, and 12-inch pipes).

- Use a comma in numbers larger than 999: 12,000, 9,000, 800.

- Use Arabic (1, 2, 3), not Roman (I, II, III), numerals for figures, illustrations, and tables.

- Change Roman numerals to Arabic in references, even when Roman numerals are used in the work itself: (Example: USEPA Region 10, Phase 3).

4.11 Parallelism

This is an important—albeit confusing—topic for technical writers, especially since we use so many lists. Basically, the elements in a list must all have the same grammatical structure. They must each flow individually from the introductory sentence. Make sure all the elements in a bulleted list, for example, are parallel to each other. If you begin one item with a verb, for example, all items must begin with a verb. The beginning of a list is the most important part; if necessary, it is acceptable to add additional elements to one or more items (see final example, below).

Incorrect: I like to do the following: flying an airplane, ride a bicycle, and shooting a gun.

Correct: I like to do the following: flying an airplane, riding a bicycle, and shooting a gun.

Incorrect: My dog is old, ugly, and he has a disease.

Correct: My dog is old, ugly, and diseased.

Incorrect: Approximately half the landfill was open to the public, and 25 percent was under development.

Correct: Approximately 50 percent of the landfill was open to the public, and 25 percent was under development.

Incorrect:

- Drill borings
- Installing wells
- Collection of samples

Correct:

- Drill borings
- Install wells
- Collect samples

Incorrect:

The objectives of this investigation were as follows:

- To determine the extent of petroleum-hydrocarbon impacted soils in the areas of confirmed impact.

- Determining the potential presence of petroleum-hydrocarbon impact to soil and water along the eastern edge of the pad.

- Collect subsurface hydrogeologic information.

- Collect such data as may be necessary, including identifying physical characteristics of the site, to support development of corrective actions and RBCLs, if warranted.

Correct:

The objectives of this investigation were as follows:

- To determine the extent of petroleum-hydrocarbon impacted soils in the areas of confirmed impact.

- To determine the potential presence of petroleum-hydrocarbon impact to soil and water along the eastern edge of the pad.

- To collect subsurface hydrogeologic information.

- To collect such data as may be necessary, including identifying physical characteristics of the site, to support development of corrective actions and RBCLs, if warranted.

4.12 References in the Text

- All that is necessary in the text is the author's last name and the year of publication (Smith, 1989). The complete information is found in the reference section. However, if you choose to give the author's full name first use or to list the title, that is acceptable.

- Use a semicolon to separate two or more references in the text (XYZ Company, 1993; USEPA, 1999).

- If the same author has more than one publication from the same year listed in the references section, use "a," "b," etc. (XYZ Company, 1999a).

- Note that commas follow the last name in our company's style (Jones, 2000).

4.13 Spacing

- Our company's style is to put one space after a period.

- There should only be one space after a comma, semicolon, or colon.

- The spacing of ellipsis points is (space) dot (space) dot (space) dot (space). Example: Mr. Rogers said that "easy children are . . . wonderful."

- The spacing of ellipsis points with an end period is (no space) dot (space) dot (space) dot (space). Example: According to NOAA, "The data are incomplete. . . ."

4.14 Spelling

- Use *Merriam-Webster's New Collegiate Dictionary* (m-w.com) as a standard spelling reference. If there is a choice of two spellings, use the first one (for example, canceled rather than cancelled).

- A list of commonly misspelled words is included in the Section 10.0 of this style guide.

- Watch for the following plurals, and remember that plural nouns take plural verbs. Singular: datum, matrix, phenomenon, schema. Plural: data, matrices, phenomena, schemas. The data are, the datum is . . .

4.14.1 Change British Spelling to American English

If you are asked to edit a British document for an American company, or vice versa, this list (Table 4-1) of the main differences between British and American spelling should make your task easier.

Table 4-1   British and American Spelling Differences

British	American
-our (vapour, colour)	-or (vapor, color)
-re (centre, metre)	-er (center, meter)
-ogue (dialogue)	-og (dialog)
-ence (defence)	-ense (defense)
-ise (minimise)	-ize (minimize)
-ising (utilising)	-izing (utilizing)
-isation (utilization)	-ization (utilization)
-isance (cognisance)	-izance (cognizance)
manoeuvred	maneuvered
learnt	learned
traveller	traveler
modelled	modeled
aluminium	aluminum
sulphide	sulfide
whilst	while
programme	program
judgement	judgment
towards	toward

American English spelling sometimes does not double the consonant at the end of a word, while British English spelling does, especially when the consonant is an "L"; for example, *travel, traveller, travelling* (U.K.) and *travel, traveler, traveling* (U.S.).

Also, note that U.S. English differs for the following (these are U.S.): single quotes inside double quotes, brackets inside parentheses.

4.15   Temperatures

- Use the numeral, the degree symbol, and either "F" or "C" for temperatures. Example: The temperature was 14 °F inside the building.

- Be consistent with using either F or C. U.S. companies will often give the temperature in Fahrenheit first, then in Celsius in parentheses, as in the following example:

  − The water temperature shall not be less than 40 °F (4.4 °C).

- The correct definitions and spellings are Fahrenheit (F) and Celsius (C). Some companies use "Centigrade" instead of "Celsius," but our company's style is to use Celsius.

4.16   Tense

In general, technical writers use present tense unless referring to past events. In those cases, use past tense. Proposals will probably also use future tense (*XYZ Company will evaluate the data*). Refer to other sources in past tense (*Smith said that . . .*). Discuss past results of tests in past tense (*One water sample was analyzed for VOCs*). Discuss final results and conclusions in present tense (*the results indicate*). Following are examples of correct tense usage:

- John Smith said, "I don't think so."

- The landfill was evaluated by Jane Doe, who said at the time, "There are clear violations here."

- Janet Smith, in *The Making of a Great Disposal Area*, wrote, "Efficiency is the most important thing."

- If the participant is finished answering the questions, the data are complete.

- Since that time, investigators from several studies have used this method.

- The CERCLA investigation includes the following. . . .

- Successfully completing site investigation or RI/FS projects has been the subcontractor's main focus since 1990.

- The group was formed to provide a core of specialists to the FAA. . . .

- The company's field staff members are trained to . . .

- Examples of site investigations XYZ Company has performed in Alaska include. . . .

- This report includes seven sections and two appendices.

- Section 1.0 contains the report introduction. . . .

- XYZ Company is recognized as a leading groundwater consulting firm.

4.17   Time

- Use a.m. and p.m. (note lowercase and periods) when included with the time: 10 a.m.

- Do not define a.m. and p.m.

- Use numerals when referring to a specific time, even if the number is less than 10. Example: The company ran the test at 3 p.m. and again at 9 p.m.

- Do not put two periods next to each other, even if a.m. or p.m. end the sentence. Example: The company ran a final test at 1 a.m.

- Do not put o'clock or :00 after the time if it is on the hour (Example: Sample collection occurred between 11 a.m. and 1 p.m.). But do use a colon and a numeral when giving specific times that are not on the hour (Examples: 2:15 p.m., 4:32 a.m.).

- If you are referring to a nonspecific time, do not use a.m. or p.m. Example: The company representatives arrived in the afternoon. But generally, in technical writing, we try to be exact, so use the correct time if you can.

4.18   Titles and Names of People

- Capitalize titles only when they directly precede a person's name or are part of an address: The source of the information was Project Manager Jane Szmanski. The project manager is Jane Szmanski. Jane Szmanski, project manager, is . . .

- Do not use a hyphen in vice president.

- In the text, give the person's full name the first mention. From then on, use Mr. or Ms. before the last name. If you are not sure of the person's gender, continue using the full name. Examples: John Smith, Mr. Smith; Sally Jones, Ms. Jones; Pat Johnson, Pat Johnson.

4.19   Unbiased Language

By now we all know we should write language that is inoffensive, but sometimes it is difficult to know what to replace words with. Sometimes the correction may seem wordy or awkward. Often the simplest way to avoid using *he/she* or *he and she* is to make the subject plural. For example, replace "An English teacher has little time to read anything except his or her students' papers" with "English teachers have little time to read anything except student papers." Modern English handbooks contain many suggestions for revising to eliminate biased language. Table 4-1 contains examples from the *Publication Manual of the American Psychological Association.*

Table 4-2   Replacing Biased Language with Unbiased Language

Replace:	With:
The client is the best judge of his counseling.	Clients are the best judges of the counseling they receive. The client is the best judge of the value of counseling.
man, mankind	people, humanity, human beings, humankind, humans
man a project	staff a project, hire personnel, employ staff
manpower	workforce, personnel, workers, human resources
woman doctor, lady lawyer, male nurse, woman driver	physician, lawyer, nurse, driver
chairman	chair, chairperson
foreman	supervisor or superintendent
Eskimos	Inuit, Aleuts (be specific)
disabled person, mentally ill person	person with a disability, person with mental illness
stroke victim, suffering from multiple sclerosis, confined to a wheelchair	individual who had a stroke, people who have multiple sclerosis, uses a wheelchair

Source: *Publication Manual of the American Psychological Association*

5.0   WRITING TIPS

The purpose of this section is to help you make your writing sharp and clear and to point out common errors to avoid, such as using clichés.

5.1   Overview

No matter what type of writing you are doing, technical or not, consider two things as most important: (1) audience, and (2) ethos (or your writer's tone; how you come across). Try to consider your audience when you write, and do not expect your readers to be experts in your subject matter or to know the definitions of the terms, acronyms, and abbreviations you are using. At the same time, consider your "ethos" by not writing "down" to your audience. You want to approach your subject matter with both respect for the readers and clarity.

Often, as a technical editor, my job is to tell the author, "This doesn't make sense to me here. Can you clarify?" I represent the "nonexpert" audience, and I try to read from this perspective, so I can tell the writer exactly where the writing might "lose" the readers.

You, as the writer, and an expert on the subject, might know what you mean, but did you really explain it to the reader in a clear, concise manner? Other questions to consider include:

- Are all tables and figures explained fully in the text before they appear?

- Do the tables make sense on their own?

- Can the reader follow your organization?

Outlines can be handy tools to use before actually writing, as discussed in Section 4.5. Personally, I prefer to make an outline before I am going to write technical material. Your outline can be just a few notes, a list of major (and perhaps minor) headings, or a full-on list of every paragraph in the document. Whatever helps you organize the material best is the method to use.

It may be necessary to go back after writing and reorganize sections. Some writers work better getting the material down quickly, and then going back and reshaping it.

If you are "stuck," or feel that your document is not flowing well, do not hesitate to ask the technical editor for help.

5.2   Getting Started

Here are some tips that may help you get started in writing your document. An English handbook also provides many ideas for beginning the writing process, outlining your ideas, and organizing your material. Therefore, if you have "writer's block," it might also be useful to look through those sections in a handbook. Here are steps to take before you begin writing:

1. Gather information and data (think about what you want to say).

2. Identify and refine your document's purpose (consider why you are going to say it).

3. Identify your audience (determine who you are going to say it to).

4. Organize your information and ideas (decide how you are going to say it).

For Step 4, it is useful to make an outline. Your outline can be changed, of course, but it will often lead you to knowing your headings and subheadings and where to put specific material in your document. A writer might find it easier to write the outline as a Table of Contents page.

The next step is actually writing the draft. You can write sections out of order, if needed. Do not worry about grammar, punctuation, and style at this point. Just get something down.

After you have your draft written, go ahead and do your revisions. If you have time to set it aside a day, go ahead and do so. As you revise, aim to clarify, strengthen, and condense your message. Also, check the overall organization. This is also the time to go back and write the introductory material, such as the Transmittal Letter and Executive Summary, if needed in this report.

As you revise, here are some questions that might assist you:

- Does the reader know what the report, section, or paragraph is about? If not, make sure you have the topic sentences or main ideas listed first. Example: "This section evaluates the data collected from the three well sites."

- What does the audience most likely want to know? Check any materials you have (bid packet, report guidelines, previous reports, original proposal) to make sure you have provided the necessary information.

- How well organized is the document?

- Are there any gaps in logic or information?

- Is there enough supporting material (i.e., figures, tables, graphs)?

- Did you use transitional words and phrases (therefore, furthermore, for example, however, in fact, also, first, second, finally, consequently, in addition, on the other hand, next, in conclusion, as a result, in the same way, in other words, in contrast, most important, further, to summarize)?

- How well did you say it? Do you have awkward sentences? Have you checked for the following problem areas (this is also done by the technical editor): sentence structure, sentence variety, subject-verb agreement, passive voice, wordiness, misuse of pronouns, misplaced modifiers, faulty parallelism, poor organization, and poor formatting? Use your handbook or this style guide for suggestions on improving these areas.

- Did you leave anything out that is essential to fulfilling the requirements of the document?

- Did you include information that is not relevant?

- Did you use specific, concrete language? Can a nonexpert read your document?

- Did you avoid jargon, clichés, and wordiness?

- Did you use enough headings and bullet lists to add to readability?

5.3 Active and Passive Voice

"Don't use passive voice," is probably one of those red-ink English teacher comments you sometimes saw but that was never explained. Active voice is preferred because it is easier to read and to understand, so it is especially important in technical material. Basically, in the active voice, the subject comes first. Another way to look at it is that the subject does the acting.

ACTIVE: The contractor evaluated the data.

In passive voice, the subject is acted upon. The reason this is a problem is that it is wordy and harder to follow.

PASSIVE: The data were evaluated by the contractor.

5.4   Be Specific

Technical writers should be as clear and specific as possible, avoiding vague language. Therefore, if you are seeing words like "many, some, a few" in a document, it probably needs revising. Instead of writing "a very high concentration," for example, give the exact measurement. Give the depth of a test pit rather than just calling it "shallow" or "deep." Instead of merely saying something is "contaminated," provide the reader with the amount by which the standard is exceeded and specifically name the compounds involved. Instead of saying something is satisfactory, state exactly which standards or regulations it meets.

5.5   Clichés

Avoid clichés like the plague; they are overused expressions that have lost their meaning. Even if you are blind as a bat, you can see a cliché for what it is: nothing.

5.6   Jargon

One of the main goals of technical writers is to make text clear and simple. One of the ways this is done is by replacing jargon with simple, clear language. Jargon is technical vocabulary, and it is often not necessary. One of the best things to happen to technical writing in the last 20 years is the elimination of jargon and the increase in readability of documents. Writing jargon or extra words (such as this example from APA: "monetarily felt scarcity" instead of "poverty") prevents readers from understanding the text. Here is an example from another company's style guide:

> Winston Churchill, facing Hitler's armed forces in 1940, said to Americans, "Give us the tools, and we will do the job." He did not say, "Supply us with the necessary

inputs of relevant equipment, and we will implement the program and accomplish its objectives."

Table 5-1 contains examples of jargon and ways to correct them.

Table 5-1   Simplifying Jargon

Replace	With
adjacent to	next to, beside, near, adjoining
atop	on
currently	now
per your request	as requested
observed	saw
presently	now
prior to	before
with regard to, relating to	about, for, of
reside	live
residential structure	residence
stated	said
subsequent to	after
upon	on
usage	use
utilize	use
with respect to	about

Source: *Chicago Manual of Style*

5.7   Sentence Errors

Comma splices, fragments, and run-on sentences are the three most common sentence errors. Any English handbook contains detailed definitions of each of these, but here are examples for your reference.

Comma Splice: A comma splice has a complete sentence before the comma, it also has a complete sentence after the comma.

How to correct: Use a period or a semicolon instead of a comma, or add a coordinating conjunction after the comma (and, but, or, for, so, yet).

Fragment: An incomplete thought. Fragments are unfinished because. All sentences need, at a minimum. A subject and a verb.

<u>How to correct</u>: If it sounds incomplete, it is probably a fragment. Revise the sentence.

<u>Run-ons</u>: Run-on sentences are two sentences crashed together they have no punctuation in between them.

<u>How to correct</u>: The easiest way to correct run-on sentences is to put a period or semicolon in between the two sentences.

5.8   Vague Terms

Try to avoid using "it" and vague pronoun references. State exactly who or what you mean.

CONFUSING: Columbia Analytical Services gave the results to XYZ Company. It then gave the results to the client's representatives. They . . .

CLARIFIED: Columbia Analytical Services gave the results to XYZ Company. XYZ Company gave a copy of the results to the client, Company A. Company A then . . .

Also, note that a company is singular, so you would not use "they" when referring to a company. This is where you will sometimes use "it," but make sure your text is clear on who or what "it" refers to.

5.9   Wordiness

Technical writing should be "tight" and clear. If you can use one word instead of three or four, do so. The main problem with wordiness is that it makes the text hard to read. Table 5-2 shows some shorter alternatives to wordy phrases such as using "for" instead of "for the purposes of."

Another way to eliminate wordiness is to avoid redundant phrases. In the following examples from APA, the italicized words are redundant and should be eliminated: *one and* the same, in *close* proximity, *completely* unanimous, *period of* time, summarize *briefly*, the reason is *because*, has been *previously* found, small *in size*, *a total of* 68 participants, *both* alike, four *different* groups.

Table 5-2   Eliminating Wordiness

Wordy Phrase	Better
a 7-year period	7 years
a large number of	many

Wordy Phrase	Better
ahead of schedule	early
as to whether	whether
at this point in time	now
based on the fact that	because
blue in color	blue
close proximity	proximity
conduct interviews with	interview
consensus of opinion	consensus
constructed in two levels	two-story
contained within	in
designated, termed, named as	designated, termed, named
developed for residential use	residential
divided into four quarters	divided into quarters
during the time that	while, when
end product	product
few in number	few
fine-grained in texture	fine-grained
first priority	priority
for the purpose of assessing	to assess
for the purpose of	for, to
future potential	potential
immediately adjacent to	next to, beside, adjoining
in a shingle-type method	like shingles
in advance of	before
in excess of	over, exceeding
in order to accomplish	to accomplish
in proximity to	near
in regard to, in relation to	regarding, about, of
in the event that	if
in the near future	soon
in the vicinity of	near, about
infiltrate through	infiltrate
integral part	part
is in a muddy condition	is muddy
is to be established	will be established

Wordy Phrase	Better
it is *Company*'s understanding	*Company* understands
may, might possibly	may, might
of a similar nature, similar in nature	similar
on a monthly (weekly) basis	monthly (weekly)
on an as-needed basis	as needed
performed a site reconnaissance	reconnoitered (the site)
prior to the collection of samples	before samples are collected
results so far achieved	results so far
the present study	this study
there were several students who completed	12 students completed
to the point that	enough, sufficiently
topographic features	topography
were used for the storage of	stored
work, tasks performed	work, tasks

Source: *Chicago Manual of Style*

5.10   Words to Avoid for Liability Reasons

Try to avoid overstating or overpromising. Be careful with word selection. Make sure if you use the following words and ones similar to them that you are not promising or saying too much: all, none, always, never, any, eliminate, stop, equal, guarantee, warrant, certify, ensure, insure, best, highest, maximum, minimum.

There are other words available in this rich English language that should serve your purposes just as well, depending on the context, such as sufficient, typical, facilitate, monitor, equivalent, similar, limit, reduce, recommend, and review.

Here is an example: Instead of *XYZ Company guarantees to provide the client with the best choice*, write *XYZ Company will advise the client on the most appropriate action.*

6.0   STANDARD DOCUMENT FORMATTING

Overall, most companies prefer block format for all technical documents. Block format means that paragraphs are single spaced (or perhaps 1.15 as shown on Figure 6-1, below), with a full paragraph space above (also shown on Figure 6-1; in this case, I inserted 12 points above each paragraph and 0 points below; this would be standard when the font size for "normal" text in the document is also 12 points). Headings should also have 12 points above and 0 points below.

Most companies seem to prefer left justification for reports and other documents as well. This is easier to read. However, full justification can look more professional, so this is your decision.

There should only be one space after a period, colon, or semicolon. This changed since the "typewriter days," when two spaces were called for after a period. Now it is easy to search and replace two spaces with one throughout an entire document.

I have formatted the book form of this document to model what I suggest:

- Times New Roman 11-point font for normal text.

- Arial bold font for headings

- One space after periods, commas, and semicolons.

- Block format (11 points above each single-spaced paragraph).

- Figure and table captions before the figure and table, and always referenced in the text before they appear. (Note that some disagree with me on this and still put the figure captions below, or after, the figure. As an editor, I accept and use the company's style I am working with. But I prefer to have the caption before the figure so that I can add notes below the figure and so that a short title can be used that will be included in the automated Table of Contents.)

Figure 6-1   Paragraph Spacing for Technical Documents

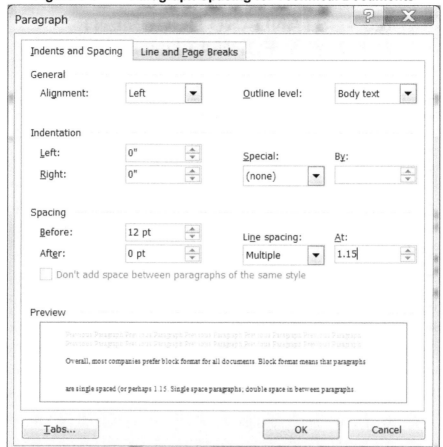

6.1   Memorandum

The standard format for memoranda is as follows:

Margins: 1 inch from top, bottom, and both sides.

Justification: Memos are fully justified.

Font: Text font is Times New Roman 11 points.

Use your company's stationery.

Introductory material: The template has the necessary information in the following order:

>Date:
>
>To:
>
>From:
>
>Subject:

Signature: Memos are not signed.

Spacing: single-spaced paragraphs with a double space between each paragraph.

End: At the end of a memo, always include the following:

>Attachments
>
>Enclosures (if any)
>
>cc: file (and any other names or places copies are going)

Length: A memo should only be one or two pages; if more than one page, consider using a letter format instead.

6.2   Transmittal Letter

A transmittal letter is sometimes included in the front matter of a lengthy (40 or more pages) report. Here are some features of the transmittal letter:

- A letter is usually one page. Short one-page letters usually have three paragraphs: introduction, body, and closing.

- The language is not technical.

- The letter documents when the report was sent, how it was sent, to whom it was addressed, how many copies were sent, and who was responsible for preparing the report.

- A letter does not use acronyms and abbreviations.

- The letter is addressed to a specific person (Dear Mr. Jones:).

- Distribution is noted on the bottom left (cc.).

- The letter also clarifies if it is a draft report, and, if so, when comments are due back and how.

- The letter indicates, if it is a draft, what is missing from the report (if anything) and when the missing information will be available.

- The letter closes by thanking the client and using the word "Sincerely,".

6.3   Standard Report

6.3.1   Document Organization

The standard document contains the following elements in this order:

- Title page

- Any preface materials (such as a transmittal letter)

- Table of Contents

- List of Appendices

- List of Figures and Tables

- List of Acronyms and Abbreviations

- Section 1.0 Executive Summary

- Section 2.0 Introduction

- Other sections, leading up to the Conclusions and Recommendations Section

- References

- Appendices

6.3.2   Spacing and Text Fonts

- Use single space text.

- Use Times New Roman 11 point font.

- If we use 11-point font, set "normal" style for 11 points before each paragraph for block paragraphing. If we use 12-point font, set normal for 12 points above (or before) each paragraph.

- Use only one space after a period, semicolon, or colon.

- Text should be left justification; shorter company documents may be fully justified.

6.3.3 Section Headings

Each section contains up to five levels of headings, which are formatted as follows:

- Caps, centered, bold, Arial 14, NUMBER AT LEFT IS 4.0

- All caps, left justified, bold, Arial 12, NUMBER AT LEFT IS 4.1

- Upper and lowercase, left, bold, Arial 11, NUMBER AT LEFT IS 4.1.1

- Upper and lowercase, number is indented .5 (1 tab), no bold, italic, Arial 10, NUMBER AT LEFT IS 4.1.1.1

- Fifth-level heading. Italics, Arial 10, underlined, DON'T USE NUMBER AT LEFT

The Table of Contents should be formatted so that only headings 1 through 3 are shown there.

Title Page

The title page should include the following:

- Report title

- Type of report (interim, internal, progress, draft, final)

- Contract, delivery, and job order numbers

- Date

- Client (Prepared for) name and address

- Client logo if available

- Company Name (Prepared by) name and address

- Terra logo

Table of Contents Page

- The header, **TABLE OF CONTENTS**, should be centered and bold.

- Items in the Table of Contents (TOC) should be all caps or initial caps, just as they appear in the text headings.

- No bold or underscores are used in the TOC.

- Second and third-level headings are indented.

- TOCs use up to third-level headings.

- Multivolume reports should each have their own individual TOCs.

List of Tables and Figures

- Use the heading "**LIST OF TABLES AND FIGURES**" all bold and caps at top of the page.

- Begin the List of Tables and Figures on a separate page from the TOC.

- Numbering is handled with hyphens: Figure 1-1.

- Items are in upper/lowercase (title case), no bold.

- If you use the caption command correctly in the text, you should never have to type in the titles and page numbers; just insert the Table of Contents, Tables, and then the Table of Contents, Figures.

List of Appendices

- The List of Appendices (if needed) is placed after the List of Tables and Figures. If it fits, it can be on the same page as the List of Tables and Figures (see example, next page).

- Use the following format for the Appendices TOC:

LIST OF APPENDICES

Appendix A   Title Here

Appendix B   Title Here

- Note that no page numbers are listed for the List of Appendices since they do not actually have page numbers. If they are lengthy documents of themselves that do include page numbers, number each page as A-1, A-2, etc. for Appendix A, and B-1, B-2, etc. for Appendix B.

List of Acronyms and Abbreviations

- Our company places the acronyms list at the front of the document, between the TOC and the Executive Summary. (Some documents are different; for example, Site Technical Practices [CRTs and STPs] include the Abbreviations and Acronyms as Section 4.)

- All acronyms used in the report, including in figures, tables, and appendices, must be included.

- Use the acronyms and abbreviations list in Section 13.0 of this style guide for guidance on capitalization and spelling.

- Be sure the entries are in alphabetical order.

Executive Summary

- Reports more than 40 pages should have an Executive Summary. It is helpful to the reader to have an Executive Summary even if the report is shorter than 40 pages.

- The Executive Summary states the purpose and nature of the investigation; provides a brief account of the approach used; and includes the major results, conclusions, and recommendations.

- The Executive Summary has its own page numbers in the format "ES-#," as in ES-1, ES-2, etc. This emphasizes that the Executive Summary can stand alone.

- Acronyms are defined in the Executive Summary as if it is a separate document that will stand on its own. Do not use them heavily.

- Though unusual in an Executive Summary, if you include Tables or Figures, number them as follows: Figure ES-1.

Report Pages

- Each main section begins on a right-hand page.

- Page numbering is based on the section. For example, page 3-2 means Section 3, page 2.

- Documents are normally printed on both sides of the page if the report is longer than 50 pages.

- Blank pages may be necessary when there is an 11x17 (foldout) figure or table because the foldout must begin on an odd-numbered page. The page after the foldout is also blank. Both blank pages are still counted in page numbering, however.

- Text font is 12 pt. Times, no bold.

- Standard practice for reports is full justification.

- Reports are usually printed on 8.5- x 11-inch white paper, single column.

- Report headings are usually 1.0, 1.1., 1.1.1, 1.1.1.1. Most companies prefer no number on heading levels 5, 6, etc. The figures below show the general and the outline number settings for Headings 1 and 2 in Microsoft Word (your preferred font type and size might be different than Arial 16 bold as I have for Heading 1, shown on Figure 6-2).

Figure 6-2   Heading 1 General Guidelines

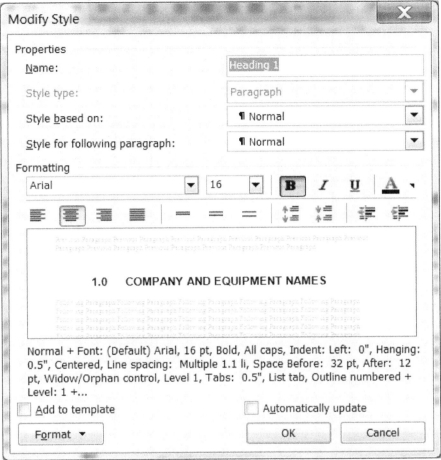

Figure 6-3   Heading 1 Outline Number Settings in Word

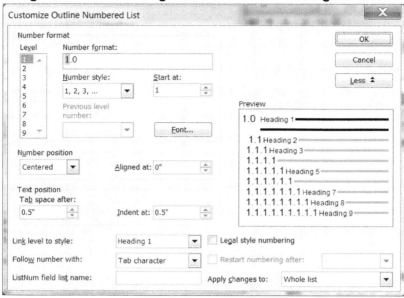

Figure 6-4   Heading 2 Outline Number Settings in Word

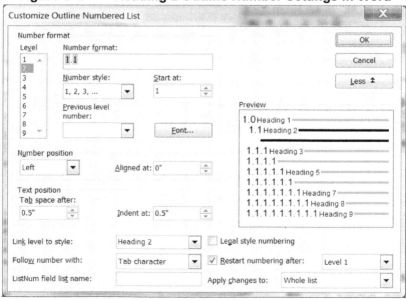

If you do not have a report template already, Wordsworth LLC (www.wordsworthwriting.net) sells report and proposal templates, as well as numerous other templates, with the heading and other styles already created and instructions inserted. The same documents, as well as thousands of government and business forms, can be purchased at Forms in Word (www.formsinword.com).

Figures and Tables

- Tables and figures are numbered according to the overall sections they are in. The second number has nothing to do with the subsections (second-, third-, and fourth-level headings); it is based on the table's order in that section. Therefore, Table 3-3 is the third table in Section 3 of the report.

- Capitalize the words *table* and *figure* only when they are used with a specific number (Table 4-4, the table).

- Use a hyphen, not a period, to separate table numbers (Table 5-7).

- Tables and figures appear after the first mention, either on the same page after the text mention or on the following page. They must be referred to in the text. Example: Figure 4-2, Site Location, identifies four areas of concern.

- Figure and table fonts are as follows: Arial 10, bold, centered. Then insert a tab before typing the title in title case (the reason for the tab instead of spaces is that it looks nicer in the Table of Contents). Table 6-1 and Figure 6-5 are examples.

Table 6-1   Cook Inlet Survey Data – 2002

Title Here – Bold and Centered	Title Here – 10 pt.	Title Here
Text in this column is usually left justified	Text in all other columns is usually centered	Text – All text is 10 pts.
Text	Text	Text
Text	Text	Text

Title Here – Bold and Centered	Title Here – 10 pt.	Title Here

Notes:
1. Always include definitions to all acronyms and notes below in smaller, indented font. Here I used 8 pt. font, Arial, no bold, left justified.
2. Note that the cells are merged here, and only the top border shows. Or you can include the notes below the table, and not within a cell.
3. Always "repeat" the header row, in case the table goes to a second page.

Key:
ADEC   Alaska Department of Environmental Conservation
USEPA   U.S. Environmental Protection Agency

Figure 6-5   Crevasse Moraine Trails

Notes:
1. I prefer to put figure captions above the figure, the same as table captions, so that I can have room for notes below a figure. I also prefer the look of the short figure captions that look nice in the Table of Contents.
2. Some companies prefer to add a third caption type, Photo, instead of using the word "Figure" for photographs.
3. I create a style called Table Notes that is smaller than the text and caption font and is set .2 spaces in, so that it is indented beneath the table. It has 2 points space before and 0 after. I use this same style for the blank paragraph under each figure and table (or after the last note if there are notes).

References

The format of references is a stylistic matter. There is no right or wrong (unless you are writing for a certain agency or company that has its own style guide). It may seem that there are almost as many reference styles as there are books. The main point is to be consistent—both throughout a document and throughout a company.

I prefer to base my references on *Chicago Manual of Style*, with some slight changes based on the hundreds of companies I have edited for. However, there are excellent online sources on Chicago Manual of style (such as this one for government citations at http://library.bowdoin.edu/help/chicago-gov.pdf or this one on general citations at http://www.chicagomanualofstyle.org/tools_citationguide.html), so Chicago might be a good one to follow). Within a month's time, I might use 10 different references styles, depending on what the client's needs are. Government agencies often have their own style guidelines; specific companies have their own style guides; academic writing has its own preferences [MLA, APA, etc.); newspapers and magazines might use AP or Chicago or their own guides). I believe the references sections is the most difficult part of a report because to find out what that particular company's preferences are and then to make all the entries (which can sometimes be in the hundreds) consistent are tricky. I also need (if the client understands the time involved in doing this correctly) to check every link to make sure it works and the spelling of titles and authors, as well as the dates, to be sure they are accurate.

My in-text citations usually just include the author (or agency) and the year. Whether or not to use a comma in between is again your choice, but be consistent; if the company has no preference, I leave out the commas, as in these examples: (Abrams 2012) (USFS 2014) (Coletta and Nagy 2014).

6.3.3.1.1 General Guidelines for References Section

Below are some overall guidelines to follow if your company does not have its own references style. The main point to keep in mind is to be consistent throughout your document. The main thing is to remember to be consistent. Your readers need to be able to find your references, if needed, so give them enough information to do so.

Entries should be alphabetically arranged by author's last name (first author listed in original text). If there is no author, list under the title. The order and description within entries are as follows:

1.   Author(s) or editor(s). Spell out the names of authors and editors in the text as they appear on the title page of the document. Avoid using "et al." (which stands for "and others") in this list unless there are more than six authors' names; reserve et al. for the text when there are more than three authors.

2.   Date. List the year of publication or "n.d." if there is no date available. If there are two or more reports by the same author in the same year, add a, b, c, etc. to the date in both text and list.

3.   Title. Titles are typed in capital and lowercase letters (title case). Titles are either italicized, placed within quotation marks, or typed with no italics or quotation marks according to the following rules:

  —   Books and reports. Italicize titles of all separate, freestanding, printed publications. Use standard capitalization rules, and spell out titles completely.

  —   Journal articles, papers in proceedings, and manuscripts in collections. Titles of material contained within larger documents are put in quotation marks; the name of the larger work is italicized and spelled out in full.

  —   Regulations and statutes. Titles of regulations and statutes are typed with no underline or quotation marks.

4.   Editor, if entry by author.

5.   Symposium or proceedings dates and locations in parentheses, if not part of the title.

6.   Volume number.

7.   Government or agency report number.

8.   Mention of draft status, if applicable.

9.   Revision or edition number.

10. Publisher.

11. Location of publisher (if a book). Use the two-letter U.S. Postal Service codes for state names. Publisher and location are not required when referencing a periodical (journal or magazine).

12. Page numbers (if an article). Insert the inclusive page numbers for articles within journals, proceedings, and technical reports,

preceded by "pp." if more than one page, or by "p." if only one page.

13.   Month (and day, if available), if needed to distinguish between drafts, etc.

14.   Web site accessed month, day, year: full link (if applicable).

6.3.4   *Sample References Section*

Note: These examples are in the style I use when a company has no preference; they aren't exactly *Chicago Manual of Style*, but close to it, and based on the list in Section 6.12.1 of this document.

Alaska Administrative Code. 2003. 5 AAC § 75.222 Policy for the Management of Sustainable Wild Trout Fisheries. Juneau, Alaska.

Alaska Department of Environmental Conservation (ADEC). 2012. *Alaska DEC User's Manual. Best Management Practices for Gravel/Rock Aggregate Extraction Projects: Protecting Surface Water and Groundwater Quality in Alaska.* Prepared by Shannon & Wilson, Inc. September. Web site accessed December 17, 2014: http://dec.alaska.gov/water/wnpspc/protection_restoration/bestm gmtpractices/Docs/GravelRockExtractionBMPManual.pdf.

Alaska Department of Fish and Game (ADF&G). 2014. Subsistence Regulations. Web site accessed August 14, 2013: http://www.adfg.alaska.gov/index.cfm?adfg=subsistenceregulati ons.main.

Alaska Energy Authority (AEA). 2012a. Renewable Energy Fund Round 6. Web site: http://www.akenergyauthority.org/RE_Fund-6.html. July.

Alaska Energy Authority (AEA). 2012b. Power Cost Equalization. Web site: http://www.akenergyauthority.org/programspce.html

Alaska Energy Authority (AEA). 2010. Alaska Energy Plan Community Database. Web site: http://www.akenergyauthority.org/alaska-energy-plan.html

Gill, A.B., and M. Bartlett. 2010. *Literature Review on the Potential Effects of Electromagnetic Fields and Subsea Noise From*

Marine Renewable Energy Developments on Atlantic Salmon, Sea Trout and European Eel. Scottish Natural Heritage Commissioned Report No. 401.

Institute of Social and Economic Research (ISER), University of Alaska Anchorage. 2012a. Internal Publications Database Search. Web site: http://www.iser.uaa.alaska.edu/publications.php?id=1518.

Institute of Social and Economic Research (ISER), University of Alaska Anchorage. 2012b. *Alaska Fuel Price Projections 2012-2035.* ISER Working Paper 2012.1 and Microsoft Excel Spreadsheet Price Model. July.

National Fire Protection Association. 2008. National Electrical Code. (NFPA70). Quincy, MA: National Fire Protection Association.

National Marine Fisheries Service (NMFS). 2013. *2013 Steller Sea Lion Protection Measures for Groundfish Fisheries in the Bering Sea and Aleutian Islands Management Area.* Preliminary Draft EIS/RIR/IRFA. March. Web site accessed August 13, 2013: http://www.npfmc.org/protected-species/steller-sea-lions/.

Person, D.K., and A.L. Russell. 2009. "Reproduction and Den Site Selection by Wolves in a Disturbed Landscape." *Northwest Science.* 83(3): pp. 211-24.

Person, D.K., M. Kirchhoff, V. Van Ballenberghe, G.C. Iverson, and E. Grossman. 1996. *The Alexander Archipelago Wolf: A Conservation Assessment.* USDA General Technical Report PNW-GTR-384.

Piatt, J.F., N.L. Naslund, and T.I. Van Pelt. 1999. "Discovery of a New Kittlitz's Murrelet Nest: Clues to Habitat Selection and Nest-Site Fidelity." *Northwestern Naturalist.* 80: pp. 8-13.

U.S. Fish and Wildlife Service. 1985. *Habitat Suitability Models and Instream Flow Suitability Curves: Chum Salmon,* by S.S. Hale, T.E. McMahon, and P.C. Nelson. Biological Report 82 (10, 108). August.

6.4 Proposals

Proposals are a marketing tool, and therefore we can have a bit more flexibility as far as formatting goes. In general, use the same formatting as the report. That can be fine for a proposal as well. If it is agreed to by the writer, editor, and project manager, such formatting changes such as columns, headings with color, text boxes featuring quotes from clients and advantages to using our company, and changes in fonts may be used. No more than two or possibly three (say, for tables) fonts should be used within one document.

6.5   Resumes

There are four standard resumes used by our company. Brief descriptions of these follow. As soon as you begin working here, you should write your resumes (in all four formats) and give them to the technical editor for editing and formatting. Also, if you already work for our company, you should update your resume at least every 6 months and give your changes to the technical editor.

6.5.1   Resume: Standard Long Version

- Treat each resume as a separate document. This means it should stand on its own, so all acronyms should be defined first use.

- Long resumes can be two or more pages.

6.5.2   Resume: Short Version

- Treat each resume as a separate document. This means it should stand on its own, so all acronyms should be defined first use.

- The short version is usually one page; two pages can be used if necessary.

6.5.3   Resume: One Paragraph

- These are used in proposals as well as on our Web site.

- Remember to update them frequently and give your changes to the technical editor.

6.5.4   Resume: SF330 Form

- For certain government proposals, we are required to use what is called the SF330 form. The font size is usually 10 points.

- There are certain standard sections to each SF330 form. (This form is available in Microsoft Word from www.formsinword.com.) A sample resume page from Forms in Word's/Wordsworth's "Sample SF330 Form Filled Out" is shown as Figure 6-6.

Figure 6-6 Sample SF330 Resume Page

E. RESUMES OF KEY PERSONNEL PROPOSED FOR THIS CONTRACT
(Complete one Section E for each key person.)

12. NAME	13. ROLE IN THIS CONTRACT	14. YEARS EXPERIENCE a. TOTAL	14. YEARS EXPERIENCE b. WITH CURRENT FIRM
Darryl Rogain	Principal Architect & Quality Control	12	7

15. FIRM NAME AND LOCATION (City and State)
ROGAIN DESIGN GROUP PC

16. EDUCATION (DEGREE AND SPECIALIZATION)
- Bachelor of Architecture, University of Alaska
- Participant – ATFP Workshop, Naval Facilities Engineering Service Center, 1999

17. CURRENT PROFESSIONAL REGISTRATION (STATE AND DISCIPLINE)
- Architecture – Alaska #1874; Maryland #1232-A
- Alaska #1235; Georgia #12864
- NCARB Certificate #43996

18. OTHER PROFESSIONAL QUALIFICATIONS (Publications, Organizations, Training, Awards, etc.)

19. RELEVANT PROJECTS

	(1) TITLE AND LOCATION (City and State)	(2) YEAR COMPLETED: PROFESSIONAL SERVICES	(2) YEAR COMPLETED: CONSTRUCTION (If applicable)
a.	Indefinite Quantity Contract for Architectural & Engineering Design Services for Various Projects, Army Base, Camp Lagoon, Alaska N62470-01-D-2002	2003	2004
b.	IDIQ Contract for Architectural & Engineering Design Services for Various Projects, Army Base, Camp Lagoon, Alaska N62470-00-D-4751	2002	
c.	IDIQ Contract for Architectural & Engineering Design Services for Various Projects, Army Base, Camp Lagoon, Alaska N62470-99-D-4087	2001	
d.	IDIQ Contract for Architectural & Engineering Design Services for Various Projects at Army Base, Camp Lagoon, Alaska N62470-98-D-3895	1999	
e.	IDIQ Contract for Architectural & Engineering Design Services for Various Projects, Army Base, Camp Lagoon, Alaska N62470-95-D-4486	1999	

	(3) BRIEF DESCRIPTION (Brief scope, size, cost, etc.) AND SPECIFIC ROLE	Check if project performed with current firm
a.	Mr. Rogain was the principal architect and conducted quality control for numerous design/build projects at Camp Lagoon. Rogain Design Group provided design only on this project valued at $19.4 million. See Project #1 for complete details. Rogain's total cost was $1.2 million.	☒
b.	Mr. Rogain was the principal architect and conducted quality control for numerous design/build projects at Camp Lagoon. Complete A&E services were provided for projects totaling $3.9 million under this IDIQ contract. See Project #2 for complete details.	☒
c.	Mr. Rogain was the principal architect and conducted quality control for numerous design/build projects at Camp Lagoon. Complete A&E services were provided for projects totaling $7.56 million under this IDIQ contract. See Project #3 for complete details.	☒
d.	Mr. Rogain was the principal architect and conducted quality control for numerous design/build projects at Camp Lagoon. Complete A&E services were provided for projects totaling $10.92 million under this IDIQ contract. See Project #4 for complete details.	☒
e.	Mr. Rogain was the principal architect and conducted quality control for numerous design/build projects at Camp Lagoon. Complete A&E services were provided for projects totaling $6.074 million under this IDIQ contract. See Project #5 for complete details.	☐

7.0   USING THE REVIEWING FEATURES IN MICROSOFT WORD

To start, I make sure I change my document template or the Word file I am using so that my Track Changes Options look like the ones on Figures 7-1 and 7-2:

- Word 2003: Under Tools, Options, Track Changes, the selections should look exactly like on Figure 7-1

- Word 2007 and later: Under Review, Track Changes, Change Tracking Options, make your selections match Figure 7-2.

Since the default has some oddities, you might not see the edits correctly if you do not change your settings to what I have shown on Figure 7-1 (or Figure 7-2 for Word 2007).

Also, be sure you always use View, Print Layout when you view texts. Word 2003 by default opens in Reading Layout, which is not the best way to work or see edits, in my view (in fact, you can easily disable it in Tools, Options, General, by unclicking "Allow starting in Reading Layout").

Figure 7-1   Track Changes Options in Microsoft Word 2003

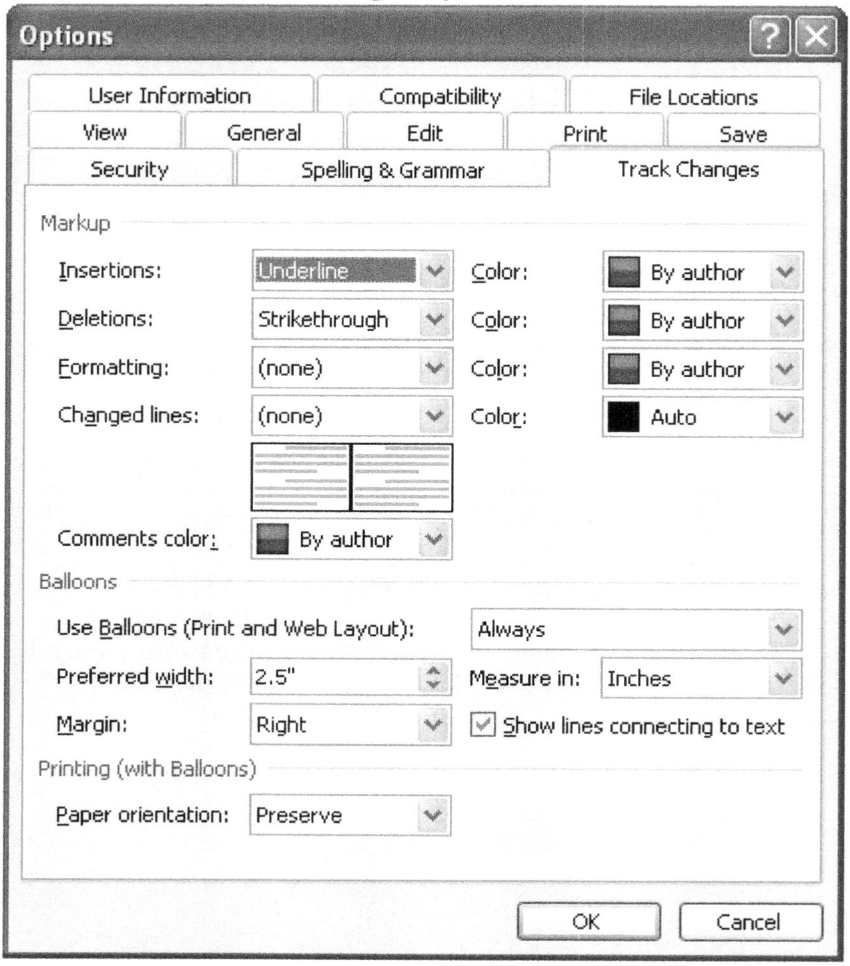

Document Style Guide

Figure 7-2   Track Changes Options in Microsoft Word 2007

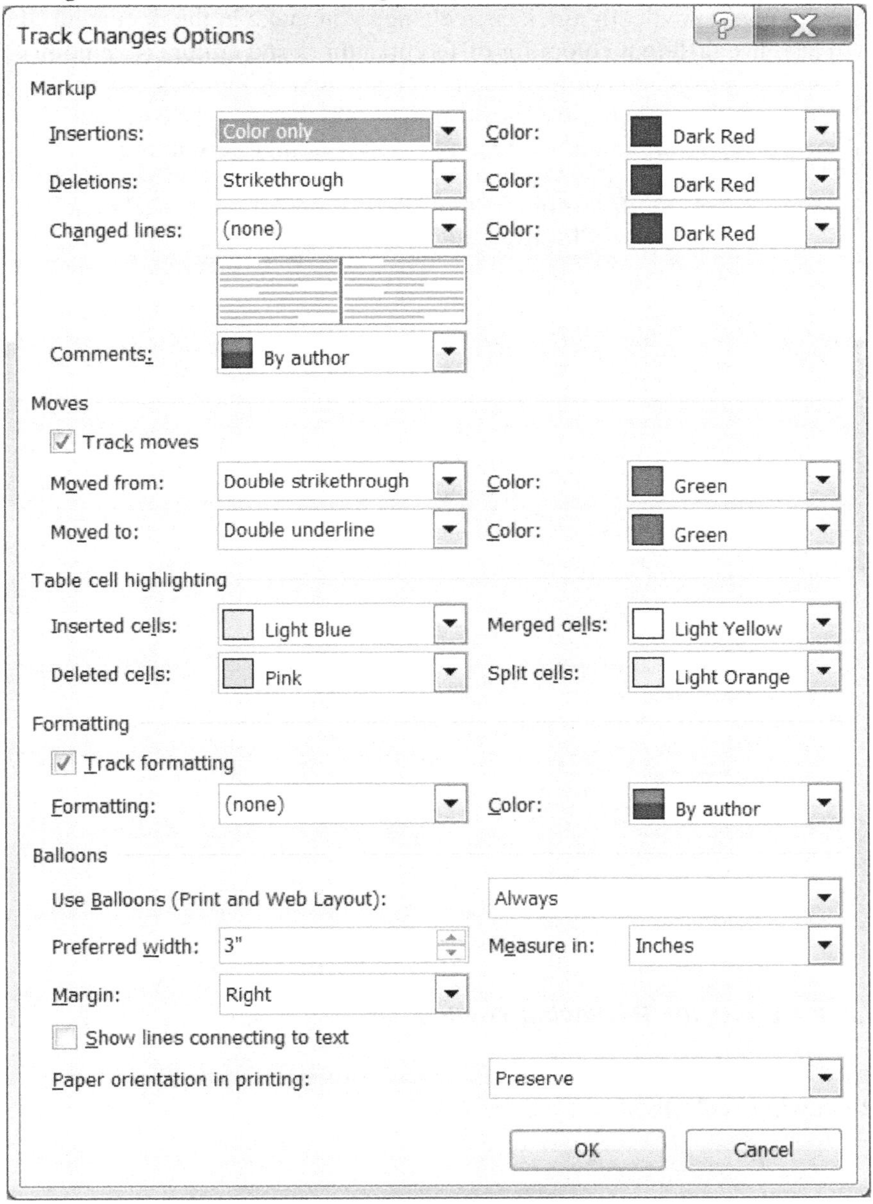

7.1   Using Track Changes

"Track Changes" is a feature of Word that allows each user to view

7-3

comments and revisions throughout the review process. Once enabled, Word will automatically track each change you make in the document. It will also use different colors for different authors and editors (to a point). Figure 7-3 shows a major rewrite of Web site text using track changes. Deletions and comments are shown in the right margin while the main editor's changes are in blue; a second editor's changes are in red.

Figure 7-3   Example from a Web Sited Edited with Track Changes and Comments

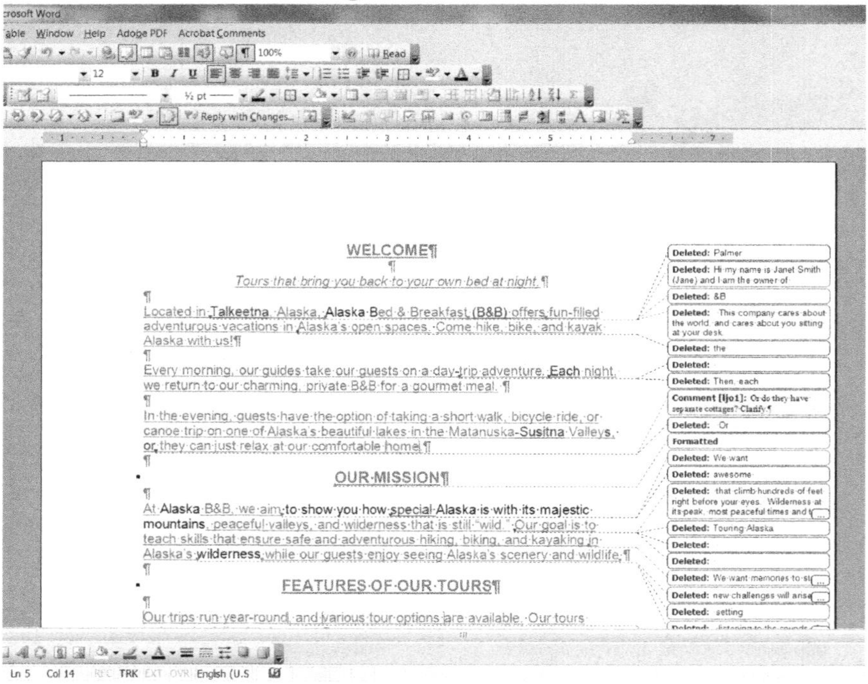

7.1.1   Using the Reviewing Toolbar

To see the reviewing toolbar, go to View, Toolbars, and be sure Reviewing is checked (see Figure 7-4).

Figure 7-4   How to Add the Reviewing Toolbar

Figure 7-5 lists some of the toolbars at the top of a Word 2003 document. See the track changes toolbar at the bottom of the toolbars (it begins with "Final Showing Markup" indented from the left, then "Show."

Figure 7-5   Microsoft Word Toolbars

The bottom toolbar is the Reviewing toolbar. To the right of "Show" are the yellow boxes with blue arrows that show you how to go from comment to comment, the yellow box with the blue checkmark that allows you to accept a change or comment (or all comments if you select the dropdown arrow next to it), and the red X that allows you to delete a comment (or all comments if you select the dropdown).

7.1.2 Accepting All Changes

Important: to the right of the yellow box with the **blue checkmark** is a **small black down arrow**. Click on this to open a feature that allows you to **accept all changes in a document**. Generally, this is what you want to do once you have glanced through the editor's changes—accept all changes. (Most editors use track changes for changes they are sure of, such as mechanics and style issues. They use the "insert comments" feature for doubts.)

Note: At certain companies, to prevent the writers from having to spend too much time reviewing edits, the editor will not use track changes for the edits she is sure about such as style, grammar, punctuation, etc. This way the writer will not be distracted and will only have to look for the comments (or areas with track changes where the editor was not 100% certain of the changes). Let the editor know if you prefer to see all changes; this is up to the writer.

Then, use the blue arrows to go to the **comments,** which are different from the track changes. (You might prefer to go through and see the comments first, before accepting all changes, in case the editor has inserted comments such as "change ok?" So that you can clearly see through the track changes what the change was.)

When you receive your file back, you can either accept or reject the changes. You can read comments three ways:

1. By hovering your mouse cursor over the highlighted text if the "balloons" are not on.

2. By looking at the comments in the comment box in the right-hand margin (if the balloons are on, which they are in this document) (see Figure 7-6).

3. By looking at the comments bar at the bottom of your screen (see Figure 7-7).

Figure 7-6   Comment in Right Margin

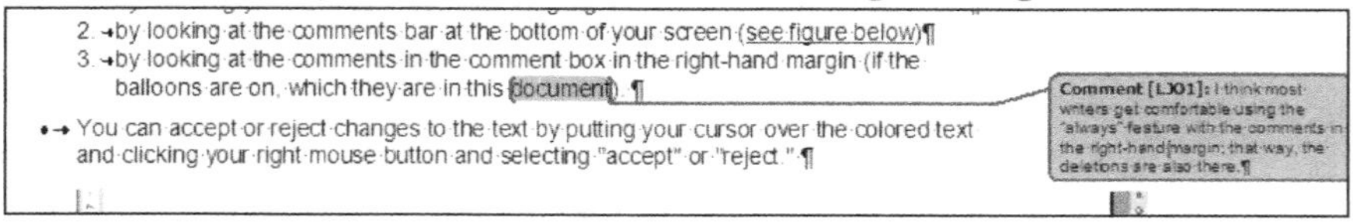

You can accept or reject changes to the text by putting your cursor over the colored text and clicking your right mouse button and selecting "accept" or "reject." You can delete the comment by clicking in the comment and then selecting the red X to delete it in the track changes toolbar.

Figure 7-7 shows how comments will be listed below the text (at the bottom of your screen) if you turn off balloons in the track changes options menu.

Figure 7-7   Comments Showing Below Document Instead of Margin

7.2   Accepting Certain Changes in Word

It might be helpful for authors to know how to accept certain changes only, so they know how to accept just my edits or formatting changes and still see the other reviewers' changes in tracked changes.

7.2.1   How to Accept Formatting Changes Only

Click the arrow to the right of Show on your reviewing toolbar (see Section 7.1.1 if you are not sure what the reviewing toolbar is), deselect everything but Formatting. Then click the arrow beside <u>Accept Change</u> and select <u>Accept All Changes Shown</u>. (Or you can hide them by just clearing Formatting from the Show menu.)

7.2.2   How to Accept Changes by One Person

Do the same process (as in Section 7.2.1) to show the edits by one person. Go to show, then reviewers, unclick all reviewers, and then just click on the ones you want to see and accept (such as Lori Jo Oswald and Eva Nagy for the technical editing). Then accept all changes shown.

7.2.3   How to Turn on Balloon Layout for Comments

Figure 7-8 is an example of two balloon comments, one from Lori Jo (LJO1 = Lori Jo's first comment in the document), and one from an editor with ME for initials (ME2 = ME second comment in the document).

Figure 7-8   Balloons in Word Showing Two Commenters

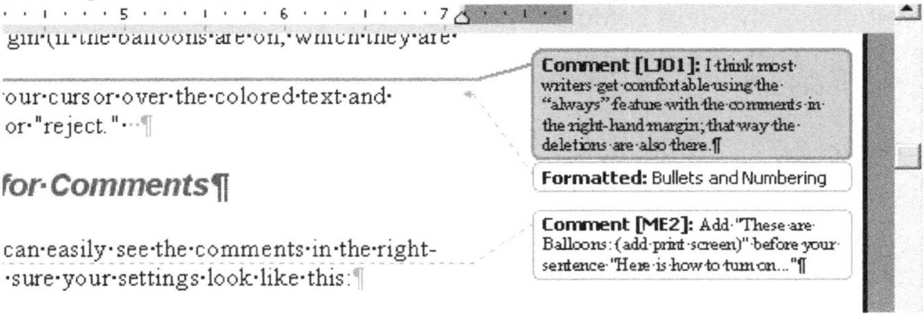

Figure 7-9 shows how to turn on the "balloons" layout option so that you can easily see the comments in the right-hand margin. Go to Tools, Options, Track Changes. Then make sure your settings look like this:

Figure 7-9   Turning on Balloons Layout

7.3   Using Comments

7.3.1   Comments Overview

The inserted comments are where the editor had some doubt, question, or requested more information. This is where you will want to either respond or ignore the comment, and then delete each comment (using the red "x" as described next).

To the right of the small down arrow is the yellow box with the **red "x" that allows you to delete a change or comment**. To the right of the red "x" is the yellow box that allows you to **insert comments**, and to the right of that is the **redlined track changes** box that allows you to turn on or off the track changes feature. Figure 7-5 shows the track changes toolbar from Word 2003. (In Word 2007 and later, just click the Review ribbon.)

In general, once you have the toolbar open on your screen, just click on the redlined "track changes" icon on the reviewing toolbar to begin inserting changes.

7.3.2   How to Attach Your Name to the Comments

- Since there may be several editors or reviewers inserting comments, it is important to attach your name to your comments in case the author has questions.
- To attach your name, go to "Tools" and select "Options." Choose "User Information" and fill in your name and your initials (see Figure 7-10). You will only have to do this once on your computer, but if you change computers, you will need to do it again.

Figure 7-10   Adding Your Name and Initials to Word Documents

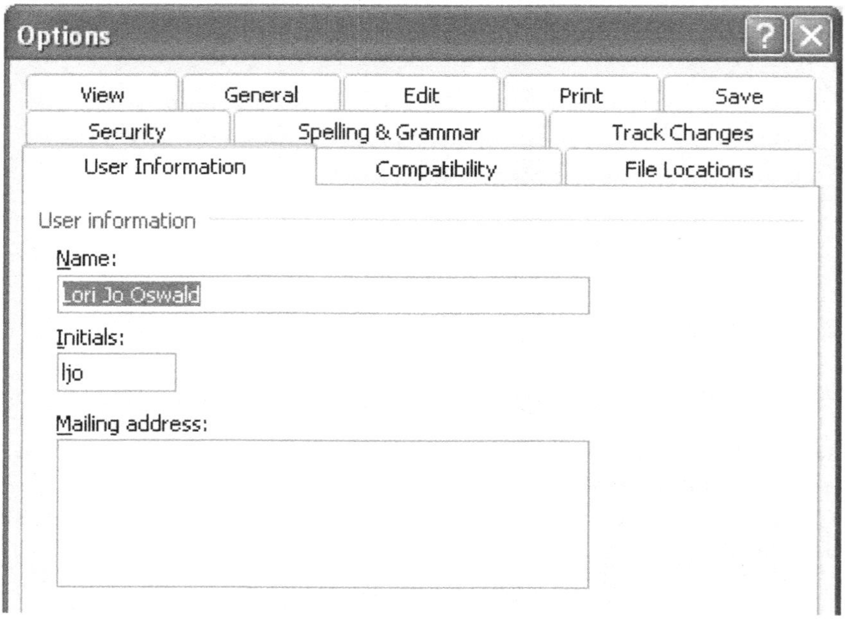

7.4   Preparing the Document for Reviewing

Make sure that you have the "Reviewing" toolbar selected so that it shows up in your toolbar. If it is not there, go to "View" and select "toolbars" and "reviewing."

To begin making comments, click on the "track changes" icon on the reviewing toolbar.

7.5   Reviewing the Document

You can now change the text directly in the document by typing or deleting and your changes will appear in color.

You can also insert a comment or question to the author by highlighting the text in question and clicking on the "Insert Comment" icon. This brings up a comment box for you to insert questions or comments.

When you actually have a comment to insert, use the yellow box (with no red or blue arrows or "x's" in it). Click the yellow box, and a comment box will be inserted at whatever point your cursor is in the text. Just type in your comment, and then click your mouse in the text to continue). Figure 7-11 is an example of a comment inserted into Word 2003:

Figure 7-11   Comment Example

When you actually have a comment to insert, use the yellow box (with no red or blue arrows or "x's" in it). Click the yellow box, and a comment box will be inserted at whatever point your cursor is in the text. Just type in your comment, and then click your mouse in the text to continue). Here is an example of a comment inserted into Word 2003.

Comment [ljo1]: The comment is here in Word 2003. If you don't see the bubble on the screen or on the printed version, go to tools, options, track changes, and be sure the box is clicked next to "show balloons in print and web layout."

Additional Information

Below is a link to a Microsoft Word training program that covers using Track Changes in Word 2003; you can Google "free training track changes in Word 2007" or whatever version you are using to find one specific to your version.
http://office.microsoft.com/training/training.aspx?AssetID=RC01160013 1033

8.0 FORMATTING AND WRITING TABLES

As with any company style, the main thing to remember with tables is to be consistent in your format. This section provides tips for formatting tables, but you might prefer a different format or shading. Still, by reading this chapter, you will understand how to make a table in Microsoft Word, and you can apply this knowledge to your own format.

8.1 Captions

The captions, or titles, of tables should be as follows:

Table 1   Title Here in Upper and Lower Case

Note the features of the above:

1. Arial 10 point bold.

2. Title in standard title case: upper and lower case.

3. Space after table title is 3 points, to separate it slightly from the table title.

4. There is no period at the end of either the table number line or the table title line.

Note that if section numbering is included instead of the 1, 2, 3, 4 format, the table and figure numbers will be different than the above example, as shown below:

Table 1-1	**Title Here**
Table 1-2	**Title Here**
Table 1-3a	**Title Here**
Table 1-3b	**Title Here**

8.2 Table Numbering

The numbering of the tables and figures should be consistent throughout the document and will depend on the numbering used in the main document.

8.2.1 Alphanumeric Numbering System

Some government agencies prefer alphanumeric numbering (I.A, I.A.1, I.A.1.a., etc.); in this case, the numbering of the table starts with the main section number where it is first mentioned in the text, followed by a period, followed by the section letter where it is first mentioned in the text (i.e., Table II.A), followed by the table number (determined by the order of the tables). Here are some examples:

- II.A-1, II.A.2, II.A-3

- III.C-1, III-C-2

The writer or editor might also choose to number related tables with an additional small letter, as follows: IV.1-9a, IV.1-9b, IV.1-9c

8.2.2 Numeric Numbering System

For the more traditional numbering system, which uses numbering only (i.e., 1.0, 1.1, 1.1.1, 1.1.1.1), the tables and figures are numbered by the section that they appear in followed by a hyphen, followed by the number (which is determined by order). Here, as an example, are the first five table numbers from Section 2.0 of a report:

Table 2-1

Table 2-2

Table 2-3

Table 2-4

Table 2-5

Note that for this method, the table (and figure) numbers only use two levels of numbering; it does not make a difference whether the tables appear in a first-, second-, third-, or fourth-level heading. They are still numbered in order of their textual reference. Also, no roman numerals are used. (As an example, this document uses this method for numbering sections and tables.)

8.3 Table Borders

8.3.1 Standard Borders

For most company tables, we use ½ point borders inside and outside. Some agencies or clients prefer thick borders on the outside as well as under the header row in tables:

1. For the outside border, as well as the border around the outside of the table header row(s), we use a 1½ point black border (or line).

2. For the inside of the table, we use a ¾-line border. Borders will be used around all items within a table for consistency and readability.

Table 8-1 is an example of our main borders.

Table 8-1   Standard Borders

8.3.2   Special Column Borders

A bolder line (1½ points) may be used between columns in one case: when there are multiple cells within a column, as in the following example (Table 8-2).

Table 8-2   Table Showing Bold Borders within Table Columns

Title Here	Title Here	Title Here (Days)			Title Here (Days)			Title Here (Days)		
		10	20	30	10	20	30	10	20	30

8.3.3   Special Row Borders

The heavier border (1-1/2 points) may be used between rows in one case—when subtitle rows are included (subtitle rows are described in Section 8.4.2 of this document). Note that in such a case, only the row above the subtitle row has the thicker border. See Table 8-3 for an example.

Table 8-3   Table Showing Bold Border within Table Rows

Title Here	Title Here	Title Here	Title Here	Title Here
Subtitle Here				
Subtitle Here				
Subtitle Here				

8.4   Table Shading

We use shading in several ways and in several percentages, based on the area of the table the shaded areas are in, as described below:

8.4.1   Header Rows

The main use of the heading, and probably the only use for most tables, is in the header row. This is the first (top) row of the table, which sometimes includes several cells within a column. This entire area will be shaded at 15%. Table 8-4 is an example.

Table 8-4   Header Row Shading

Table 8-5 is another example, with multiple cells within a column.

Table 8-5   Multiple Cell Shading

Title Here[1]	Title Here[2]	Title Here (Days)			Title Here (Days)			Title Here (Days)		
		10	20	30	10	20	30	10	20	30

Notes:

[1] Note that the cell alignment for the far left top row is left justified, bottom of row.

[2] Note that the cell alignment for the rest of the header rows is centered, bottom of row.

8.4.2   Shaded Rows within Table Body

This section describes the two ways shading is used within a table body: for subtitle rows and long data tables.

Subtitle Rows

For tables with subtitles (i.e., subheadings) within the table body, do the following:

1. Merge the cells for the subtitle row.

2. Use Arial 10 point bold for the subtitle font.

3. Left justify the subtitle.

4. Use 10% shading for the entire row where the subtitle is.

5. Use the bolder line (1½ points) for the border above the subtitle row.

6. The paragraph spacing is 2 points above and below the text for the subtitle row, the same as the rest of the table body and header rows.

See Table 8-6 for an example.

Table 8-6   Subtitle Row Shading

Title Here	Title Here	Title Here	Title Here	Title Here
Subtitle Here				
Subtitle Here				
Subtitle Here				

8.4.3   Data Tables Longer Than One Page

For lengthy data tables (more than one page) with no subtitles, use alternating shaded lines to separate data lines from each other, as in the following example (Table 8-7). Note that the alternate shaded lines use 5% shading, but if this does not show when printed, use 10%.

Table 8-7   Shading for Data Tables Longer Than One Page

For consistency and readability, no shading should be used except for those three reasons described above.

8.5   Table Text

Table text, generally, should have the following features:

- Font—Arial, 10 points, centered, not bolded, not italicized

- Width—Table width is across the page. Margins for table and figure pages are 1 inch from top and bottom, and 1.5 inches from left and right.

- Paragraph Spacing—Table text is single space, with a 2-point space above and below the text.

- Justification—Most table text is centered, but here are exceptions:

    - Often the left-hand column and header will be left justified.

    - In addition, if numbers or figures (money) with decimal places are used, the columns will be right justified, allowing just enough space from the right cell border to look balanced within the columns.

- Blank Cells—There should never be a "blank cell." Use either NA or -- to fill each cell where no data are listed. See Table 8-8 for an example.

- Cell Alignment—For the header row, align the cells at the bottom (in Microsoft Word, select the header row, right click, choose cell alignment, and choose the bottom centered tab). All rows are centered except, in some cases, the left row, which would be left justified (including the header).

- Note that no italics or all-capitalized words (except acronyms and abbreviations) are used in the table body (see Table 8-8).

Table 8-8   Sample "Blank Cell" Data and Notes

		--	NA	

Notes:
-- = No data are available for this sample.
NA = Not applicable.

A table font style with these features will be set up in the report and proposal templates for use by data processors, editors, and writers.

Exceptions: The table font size and table width can vary depending on need and text (see Section 8.6 for a discussion of table width). If, for example, it is possible to fit a table onto one page if the font size is changed to 9 points and the notes (as discussed in Section 8.7) are reduced to 8 point, the document processor has that freedom. Similarly, if the document processor needs to make the paragraph spacing above and below the table text 1 point instead of 2 to fit the table to one page, that is acceptable.

8.6   Table Width and Justification

In general, the table width is across the page.

Margins for table and figure pages are 1" from top and bottom, and 1.5" from left and right.

Exception: It is acceptable for narrow tables (for example, 2 to 3 columns with little text) to not use the entire page width. In that case, just narrow the column width to a bit wider than the text. See Table 8-9 for an example.

Table 8-9   Exception to Page Width for Tables

8.7   Table Notes

Table notes can come with three headings: Notes, Key, and Source, and if more than one is used, they should appear in that order.

Table notes have the following features:

- Arial, 9 point

- The first word (such as "Notes:" in Table 8-10, below) should have a 3-point space between it and the bottom border of the table.

- Left justified

- The words "Key:" "Notes:" and "Source:" will be bold (the colon is also bold).

- There is no border around the table notes section (see Table 8-10).

- Footnotes are included under the "Notes" heading.

- "Key" is used when acronyms and abbreviations need to be defined; the format is shown in Table 8-10.

- The words "Notes:" "Key:" and "Source:" appear on a separate line from the text that follows, as shown in Table 8-10.

- Periods are used for complete sentences and source listings.

- For acronym and abbreviation listings, no periods are used. An equal (=) sign is used between the acronym and the definition, as in GRO = gasoline range organics.

- Follow regular capitalization rules when defining acronyms and abbreviations. If the definition is capitalized (for example, EPA = Environmental Protection Agency), capitalize it in the Key section. If the definition is not usually capitalized (for example, PAH = polycyclic aromatic hydrocarbons), do not capitalize it in the Key section. (See Table 8-10.)

- Note that some clients prefer an equal sign (=) or an en dash with spaces between the abbreviation and the definition in the table notes (see Table 8-10). Personally, I prefer tabs, so if the company does not have its own style guide, I use tabs, as follows:

  USFWS   U.S. Forest Service

Table 8-10   Table Notes, Key, and Sources Example

Title Here	Title Here	Title Here (Days)	Title Here (Days)	Title Here (Days)
		23^1		
		45		
		62		

Notes:

Production and reserve data as of December 2000.

[1] Days estimated based on results from November 2001 sampling.

Key:

DRO = diesel range organics

EPA = Environmental Protection Agency

Source:

Griffiths and Gallaway (1982).

9.0 COMMONLY USED WORDS

The purpose of this section is to provide consistency with certain words. Is it one word or two? Is there a hyphen or not? Should it be capitalized or not? When in doubt, use *Merriam-Webster's Collegiate Dictionary* to be sure. Here are some examples from one company's documents:

- as-built (when used as an adjective preceding a noun, as in as-built survey)
- echo sounder (two words, Webster's)
- echo sounding (not in Webster's, but presumably two words based on echo sounder)
- fieldwork
- side-scan sonar (hyphen and use with the word sonar, Webster's)
- site-specific (adjective preceding noun)
- static GPS
- subbottom (not sub-bottom)

As you come across words that you think need to be included in this list (or changed), suggest them to the technical editor for future editions of this style guide.

Note: The words below are based on our client's preferences, Webster's, and government agency preferences, but your company may prefer a different spelling. If a word is not found in Webster's (www.m-w.com) as one word (such as streambank, which is listed here as one word because many clients prefer it that way; however, if the company does not have a preference, I will make it two words since it does appear in Webster's as one [i.e., stream bank]). But company style rules. Therefore, you may have your own preferences for some of these. Examples are wellfield (*well field* since not in dictionary, but often one word per company preference) and *work plan* (two words since not in Webster's, but many companies prefer workplan).

Note: Adjectives listed with hyphens only take the hyphen when they appear *before* the noun.

A

above grade (adverb: occurred
above grade)

above ground (adverb: occurred
50 feet above ground)

abovegrade (adjective: before
noun; abovegrade work)

aboveground (adjective:
aboveground tank, but: pipe was
located above ground)

absorption

accommodate

acrolein

across-bed

adapter (not adaptor)

adsorb (vs. absorb)

adsorption

aerial

air bag (noun)

air conditioning (noun)

airborne

air-cooled

airflow

airport

airstream

airtight

all right (incorrect: alright)

allocable

alluvial, alluvium

already, all ready

analog (a chemical compound
that is structurally similar to
another); otherwise, use

analogue

analytes

anemometer

anion

anisotropy, anis tropic

anticline

appendices (plural)

appendix (singular)

aquifer, aquitard

areal

areawide

auger

autoignition

autorefrigeration

autotransformer

B

back draft

back pressure (not back-
pressure unless adjective before
noun)

back up (verb)

backfill (noun), backfilled

backflow

backhoe

backlighted

backup (noun, adjective)

backwash

backwater

back welding

backyard

baffle board

baghouse

bakehouse

bar screen

bark chips

bark dust

base flow

base map

base station

baseline

base-neutral-acid

baseplate

bases (plural of basis)

basewide

basinwide

bathymetric (adjective)
bathymetrical (adjective)
bathymetrically (adverb)
bathymetry (noun)
bay water
bedrock
behavior (not behaviour)
below grade (adverb: occurred below grade)
below ground (adverb: occurred below the ground)
below-grade (adjective or noun)
belowground (adjective: belowground sampling)
bench mark (permanent elevation marker)
benchlands
benchmark (standard; point of reference)
bench-scale
biannual (occurring twice a year)
biennial (occurring every 2 years)
biocell
biodegradeable
bioremediation
bioturbated
bioventing
biweekly
block work (construction)
blow line
blow-count (noun)
blowdown (noun, adjective)
blow down (verb)
blowup (noun, adjective); blow up (verb)
bondholder
bookkeeping
borehole

bottom-land
bottommost
break down (verb)
breakdown (noun)
breakup (noun)
build out (verb)
build up (verb)
buildout (noun)
build-up (adjective)
buildup (noun)
built-up
bulldozer
buoys
buy back (verb)
buy-back (adjective: buy-back terms)
bypass
by-product

C

caliper (not calliper)
campground
canary grass
canister (Webster's prefers to cannister)
cannot
carbureted
carryover
casthouse
cataclastic
catch basin
cation
Cenozoic era
center pivot
centerline
centigrade (international term for Celsius)
chain wheel
chain-link (adjective: chain-link fence)

chain-of-custody (adjective)
change-out
Charpy
check out (verb)
check stop
checklist
checkout (noun)
checkpoint
chipboard
citywide
clayey
claypan
claystone
clean up (verb)
cleanup (adjective/noun;
cleanup equipment)
climatological
close out (verb)
closeout (adjective/noun)
close-up
coal tar
coarse-grained (adjective)
coastline
coauthor
cobbly
cocaptain
cochair
co-composting
co-containment
cofferdam
colinear
colluvium
color (not colour)
combined-sewer (adjective)
commingle
companywide
compatibility
condenser (not condensor)
connate

constant-discharge test
contaminant (noun)
contaminate (verb)
conterminous
cool down
co-own
co-owner
co-ownership
corehole
Coriolis (effect or force)
corrosion-resistant (adjective)
cost-effective (adjective)
cost-effectiveness
cost-of-service (adjective: cost-of-service fees)
coulomb
Coulomb field
Coulomb force
counter-rotate
countertop
court-ordered (adjective)
coworker
cowrite
crop out (verb)
cropland
cross connection
cross contamination
cross over (verb)
cross section
cross ties (noun)
cross-checking
crosscut
crossgradient
crossover (noun)
cross-reference
cross-sectional
curbside
cutoff (adjective: cutoff date)
cutout

D
dam site
data (plural), datum (singular)
data sets
database
datalogger
datum (singular)
dead leg
decahydration
decision maker
decision making (noun)
decision-making (adjective)
de-emphasize
deenergize
deice
deionized
-demand (peak-demand period)
-density (high-density protein)
desiccate
DEW Line
dew point
dewatered
dialogue (Webster's prefers to
dialog)
dielectric
digester
dilatancy
DoD (lowercase "o")
DOE (uppercase "O")
double up
downdip
downdropping (adjective:
downdropping slope)
downgradient
downhill
downhole
downslope
downspout
downstream (adjective or

adverb)
downtime
drain field
drain line
drainageway
drain-down (adjective)
drainpipe
draw down (verb)
drawdown (noun)
drill bit
drill head
drill hole
drill rig
drip pan
drip-proof
drivetrain (one word if referring
to automobiles; otherwise, two
words)
drive-train components
drop box (noun)
drop off (verb)
drop-box (adjective: drop-box
service)
drop-off (adjective: drop-off
items)
dry cleaning (noun), dry-clean
(verb)
dry wall
dry well
dual-phase extraction
ductwork
dump truck
dunnage
dust tight

E
earth flow
earth moving equipment
earthfill
earthwork

east side
easternmost (but east side)
echo sounder
echo sounding
ecotoxicity
ecotoxicological
electro (no hyphen or space;
combine with next word, as in:)
electrohydraulic
electromelt
E-logs
e-mail
embayment
end caps (noun)
end point
end product
end result
end seal
ensure
errata
erratum
Ethernet
evapotranspiration
ex situ (no hyphen or italics)
exceedance (not exceedence)
-exempt (tax-exempt bond)
explosionproof
extra-capacity (adjective: extra-
capacity trunks)
Extranet

F
facies (noun singular and plural)
fail-safe (adjective/noun)
falling-head test
fallout
farmland
fast track (noun)
fast-track (adjective)
fatal-flaw (adjective: fatal-flaw

analysis)
feasibility
federal
-feed (center-feed clarifier; step-
feed mode)
feed line
feed well
feedstock
feedwater
fence line
fence post
fiberglass
field crew
field screening techniques
field streaming
field worker
fieldbus
field-wide
fieldwork (noun)
fine-grained (adjective)
fine-tune
fire chief
fire control
fire department
fire drill
fire escape
fire extinguisher
fire fighting (noun)
fire pump
fire screen
fire station
fire truck
firebox
firedamp
firefighter, fireman
fire-fighting (adjective)
firefighting (verb)
firehouse
fireman

fireplug
fireproof
firesafe
firewall
firewater
firework
firmwide
fish (for plural)
fish screen
fishkill
flame ionization
flare up (verb)
flareup (adjective/noun)
flash point
flip chart
flood way
floodplain
floodwater
floor plate
floppy disk
-flow (restricted-flow issues; on-flow train)
flow line
flow path
flow rate
flow sheet
flow stream
flow top
flowchart
flowmeter
fluoride
fluvial
fly ash
-focus (deep-focus earthquake)
focused (not focussed)
follow up (verb)
follow-up (noun/adjective)
food chain
force main

forego
foregoing
forklift
formwork (construction)
fossiliferous (adjective)
freestanding
freezeback
Freon
fresh water (noun)
freshwater (adjective)
friable
front loader
front yard
front-end loader
fulfill (not fulfil)
full time (noun)
full-time (adjective: full-time equivalent)
furans
fuse holder
FY 99, FY 00

G
gas station
gas-oil (mixture)
gauge (not gage)
gauge line
gauss
gearbox
geochemical
geodetic
geologic (except U.S. Geological Survey)
geomembrane
geomorphic
Geo-probe
geotechnical
geotextile
giveaway
-glass (cast-glass ceramics)

glass-ceramic (noun and
adjective)
gneissic
-grade (at-grade floor)
-graded (well-graded roadway)
grain-size analysis
grassland
grasslike
gray (not grey)
green chain
-grid (coarse-grid receptor)
gridded
ground bed
ground cover
groundwater (except National
Ground Water Association) (but
note: surface water)

H
half-life (noun)
halocarbons
halogen
hand out (verb)
hand switch
handheld
handhold
handhole
handout (noun)
hands-on
hard copy
hard hat
head loss
head shaft
headspace
headwall
headworks
heterogeneity
high resistivity (adjective)
high-capacity production
high-level (adjective)

hillslope
HNu (brand name, portable)
hold-down (tanks)
holding time (not hold time)
holdup (delay)
hollow-stem (adjective)
Holocene
homeowner
homogeneous, homogeneity
hook hole
hookup
horsepower
hot spot
hydro (note: no hyphen after
hydro)
hydrogeology, hydrogeologic
hydropower
HydroPunch (but lowercase if
generic)
hydrotest

I
ice floes
in depth (adverb: studied in
depth)
in situ (no hyphen or italics)
inboard (adjective)
in-board (adjective: in-board
motor)
incompatibility
in-county (adjective: in-county
use)
in-depth (adjective: in-depth
evaluation)
inflow (noun)
inhomogeneous
in-house (adjective: in-house
distribution)
in-line (adjective: in-line
service)

in-place (adjective: in-place test)
in-plant (adjective: in-plant operations)
in-service (adjective: in-service testing)
installation-wide
in-stream
interbred, interbredded
interdisciplinary
interfinger
interlayered
intermittent
intermodular
Internet
ion exchange
isoctane
isotropic
iterative

J
job site
judgment
juxtapose

K
Kelvin
kerosine (component of jet fuel)
keylock
kick off (verb)
kickoff (noun)
Kjeldahl
kriging

L
label, labeled, labeling
lamina (noun singular), laminae (plural)
land clearing
landfarm
landfill (noun)

landform
landowner
landslide
land-spreading (adjective)
land-take (adjective as in land-take requirements)
large-scale
lay-up
leach field
leach line
leachate
leak-proof
leak-tight
least squares (noun plural)
leftover
-level (low-level radiation)
life cycle (noun)
life raft
life span
life-cycle (adjective preceding noun)
lignin
-like (only if preceded by double 11:likelihood
line pipe
line shaft
lineal
linear
liquefaction
lithologic (adjective)
load out (verb)
-loading (barge-loading facility)
load-out (adjective)
lockdown
lockset
logbook
lognormal (adjective)
long range (noun)
long term (adverb/noun)

long-range (adjective)
long-standing
long-term (adjective)
low-capacity tank
lowlands
low-lying (adjective)
low-permeability (adjective)
low-resistivity (adjective)
low-yield
lunch room
lysimeter

M
main line
mainframe
make up (verb)
makeup (noun and adjective)
-making (steel-making process)
man-day (use workday)
manganese
manlift
man-made
maplet
medium (noun singular), media (noun plural)
medium-grained (adjective)
medium-range missile
medium-sized
megascopic
meltwater
mesic
metasediments
meter (not metre)
Method Three (not Method 3)
micaceous (adjective)
microcomputer
micromho(s)
microorganism
microwell
midpoint

milestone
mill water
millscale
minimize (not minimise)
modeling (not modelling)
moistureproof
monitoring well
mudflow
multi (no hyphen; join with next word)
multibeam
multidisciplinary
multifamily residence
multilayered
multimedia
multipathway
multiphase
multitask
multiyear

N
nameplate
naphtha
nationwide
no-action (adjective: no-action alternative)
no-build (adjective: no-build alternative)
nonconductive
non-debt-funded (adjective: non-debt-funded project)
nondetect
nonequilibrium
nonhazardous
nonlisted
nonmarine
nonroutine
non-steady-state (adjective: non-steady-state issues)
nontoxic

nonturbid
nonvolatile
non-water-bearing
nonwettable
northernmost
northwest-southeast
northwest-trending
N-value (noun)

O
obturator
occur/occurred/occurrence
off-gas
off-line
off-load
off-loading
off-peak (adjective)
off-post or off post
off-road (adjective: off-road vehicle)
offset (noun, adjective, or verb)
offshore
off-site (adjective and adverb)
off-take (point)
oil field
oil rig
oil well
oilless
on line (in or into operation)
ongoing
on-line (adjective or adverb)
on-post or on post
onshore
on-site (adjective or adverb)
orthoclay
orthophosphate
Otto fuel (not auto)
outbuildings
outcrop (noun/verb)
outfall

output
outsource
overburden
overflow
overlap
overlie, overlay, overlain
overrun
overwinter

P
packer test, packer-tested
panelboard
parametric
parkland
part-time (adjective)
pass through (verb)
pass-through (noun)
pastureland
pebble-sized
penetrameter
per person (adjective: per person data)
per se (no hyphen or italic)
percent
percent (usually no % except in figures/tables; however, this can vary per company style)
permeability, permeable
persistent
petroleum hydrocarbon-contaminated soils
pH
phase in (verb)
phase out (verb)
phase-in (adjective)
phase-out (adjective)
phenol
photoionization
phreactic
physiography

piezometer, piezometric
pillow block
pilot-scale
pipe lay (if an adjective before a
noun, use pipe-lay)
pipe mill
pipe rack
pipe wall
pipefitting
pipeline
pipework
pitot tube
plan holder
plasterboard
playground
Pleistocene
pole yard
policyholder
policymaker
policy-making
polyethylene
polyurethane
pore water
portland cement
postaccident (adjective:
postaccident data)
post-closure
post-evalution
postmortem (adjective /noun)
posttreatment (adjective)
pot room
pothole
potliner
power line
power pack
power plant
powerhouse
powerstation
practice

pre (generally no hyphen with
pre; see Webster's to be sure)
precede
precursor
predominant (adjective)
predominate (verb)
preestablished
preevaluation
preexisting
preplanned
pressure meter
pretreatment
preventive (not preventative)
principal-in-charge
print out (verb)
printout (noun; adjective)
problem solving (noun)
process area
process water
procure/procured/procuring
project-specific (adjective)
promontory
proof-roll
propellant
pseudoclassical
pull box
pullout
pump house
pump out (verb)
pump station
pump-out (adjective before
noun)
punch list
purge-and-trap method
push-button

Q
quack grass
quantitation
quartzose (adjective)

quasi-permanent

R

radii (plural of radius)

radioactive

rail yard

railcar

railroad

railroad tracks

rain gear

rainfall

rainwater

rangeland

-rate (constant-rate test)

rate setting (noun)

ratemaking

ratepayer

read out (verb)

readout (noun)

real-time

real-time kinematic

reconnaissance

record keeping (noun)

record-keeping (adjective)

re-create (verb; to create again)

-reducing (cost-reducing measures)

reed canary grass

reequilibrated

reestablish

reevaluate

reexamine

regarding or in regard to (not in regards to)

-regulating (temperature-regulating valves)

reinstall

-related (hazardous-waste-related tasks)

remediation

reprint

reproducibility, reproducible

-resistant (corrosion-resistant metal)

resistivity

restroom

re-treat (to treat again)

re-use (adjective, as in re-use planning)

reuse (verb)

right-of-way

rinsate (not rinseate)

rinse water

riprap

riverbank

riverbed

road map

roadbed

roadway

rock fill

rockfall

roll off (verb)

roll up (verb)

-rolled (hot-rolled steel)

roll-off (adjective: roll-off box)

roll-up (adjective: roll-up shades)

-roof (flat-roof building)

rooftop (adjective: rooftop repairs)

rule making (noun)

rule-making (adjective)

rule set

run off (verb)

run on (verb)

run out (verb); run-out (noun)

runoff (noun/adjective)

run-on (adjective /noun)

run-out (noun); run out (verb)

S
salt water (noun)
saltwater (adjective)
sandbag
sandbank
sandblasting, grit
sandpack
sandpaper
-scale (large-scale operations)
scale up (verb)
scaleup (adjective /noun)
scrap yard
seawater
sedimentary
selenium
self-contained
self-feeder
self-monitoring (adjective)
semiannual
semiarid
semiconfined
semilog, semilogarithmic
semivolatile
set aside (verb)
set point
set up (verb)
set-aside (noun)
-setting, (rate-setting goals)
setup (noun)
sewer flow
sewer shed
sewerline
sheepsfoot
sheet iron
sheet metal
sheet metalwork
sheet piles
sheet steel
sheet tin

Sheetrock®
shell-like (but grasslike; check Webster's to be sure)
shipyard
shop blast
shoreline
short range (noun)
short term (adverb/noun)
short-range (adjective)
short-term (adjective)
shut down (verb)
shut off (verb)
shutdown (noun)
shutdown valve
shut-in
shutoff (adjective)
side boom
side slope
side water
side-scan sonar
siliceous
siltstone
single-family residence
single-phase (adjective)
site work
site-specific (adjective: site-specific issue)
sitewide
sledgehammer
-slope (down-slope length)
slug catcher (some companies prefer one word)
smooth sheet
smoothed-in (adjective: smoothed-in roadbed)
snakebite
snowmelt
soil gas (soil gas field survey)
soil-pore liquid

solenoid
solenoid valve
solid waste
sonar
sonication
-source (near-source well)
southernmost
southwest-northeast
southwest-trending
spark-proof
spectrometry,
spectrophotometry
split case
split-spoon sampler
-spoon (split-spoon sample)
spray head
spreadsheet
spring line
stainless steel (noun)
stainless-steel (adjective)
stand-alone (adjective stand-alone document)
standby
stand-off
standpipe
start up (verb)
start-up (adjective/noun)
state of the art (noun)
state-certified
state-of-the-art (adjective)
statewide
static GPS
-status (special-status species)
steady state (noun/adjective)
steam clean (verb)
steam generator
steel making (noun)
steel-making (adjective)
-stem (hollow-stem auger)

step-discharge test
step-down, step-up (noun/adjective)
step-drawdown test
stepwise
stop nut
storativity
storm water (noun)
straightforward
stratigraphy, stratigraphic
stream water
streambank
streambed
streamflow
strength (full-strength test)
stubout (adjective/noun)
sub (generally no hyphen; check Webster's to be sure)
subaerial
subarea
subbasin
subbottom
subcontractor
subsea
subsection
subsurface
subsystem
sulfate, sulfite, sulfitic
sulfur
sulfur, sulfuric, sulfurous
Super Sacks
Superfund
supernate
supersede (not supercede)
surface water
surficial
switch ties
switchgrass
switchyard

syncline, synclinal

T
tailwater
take off (verb)
takeoff (noun/adjective)
talus
tamper-proof
tamper-resistant
tank farm
tannin
tare
task force
task order
teamwork (noun)
tectonic
Teflon® (trademark)
telltale (a type of valve)
test pit
-tested (tightness-tested seal)
through bolt
time frame
time line
time sheet
time-consuming
timeframe
timetable
toolshed
top-of-casing (adjective)
topsoil
total Kjeldahl nitrogen
touch-up
toward (not towards)
-track (fast-track schedule)
trade name
trademark
tradeoff
trans-Alaska oil pipeline (AP style)
Trans-Alaska Pipeline System

(TAPS) (Alyeska style)
transfer/transferring/transferred/transferable/transferal
transmissivity
travel, traveled, traveling
-treated (heat-treated metals)
tremie (adjective, not verb)
trench side
troubleshooting
trunk line
trunnion
truss-joist
t-test
tubesheet
tuffaceous
turbid
turbidity
turbulent (not turbulant)
turnaround
turnaround time
turndown
twofold
two-phased (adjective)
Tyrek®

U
U.S. (not US, and never define U.S.)
U.S.C. (for U.S. Code)
ullage
ultra-high (adjective: ultra-high frequency)
ultraviolet
unconfined
unconformable, unconformity
unconsolidated
under floor (adverb: the mouse was under the floor)
under ground (adverb: the pipe was under the ground)

under water (adverb: the site
was under water)
under way (adverb)
undercut
underdeposit
underdraln
underfloor (adjective:
underfloor pipe)
underflow
underground (adjective:
underground pipe)
underlie, underlay, underlain
underlying
underrun
under-voltage
underwater (adjective:
underwater activity)
underway (adjective)
(occurring, performed, or used
while traveling or in motion:
underway replenishment of fuel)
United States (noun), U.S.
(adjective)
unsaturated
unthreaded
upbed
updip
upflow
upgradient (adjective:
upgradient well)
uphill
uplands
uppermost
uptake
upwind
usable (not useable)
EPA-approved
user friendly

V

vadose zone
Vendor
venturi
Visqueen® (not Visquine)
volatile
volumetric

W
walk through (verb)
walk-through (noun)
-wall (double-wall construction)
wallboard
wash wastes
wash water
washout
waste line
waste load
waste stream
wastewater
water body
water main
water spray
water stop
water table
water well
water-bearing (adjective)
water-bearing unit (modifier)
water-cooled (adjective)
watercourse
waterflood
waterfowl
waterline
waterpower
watershed
watertight
waterwash
waterway
Web site
weekday
weep holes

weldability
weld pack
-well (near-well transmissivity)
well bay
well house
well line
well pad
well point
well screen
well work
wellbore
wellfield
wellhead
well-known (adjective before noun)
well known (after noun)
wellpoint
wellsite
west side
westernmost (but west side)
wet well
wheatgrass
wholly owned
wind up (verb)
windblown
windbreak
windrow (row of heaped matter)
windup (adjective/noun)
wingwall
wireway
wood waste
wood yard
work area
work over (transitive verb; to work over something)
work plan
work scope
work sheet
work site

workday
workers' compensation
workflow
workforce
workload
workman
workover (adjective, as in a hydraulic workover rig)
workplace
workshop
workstation
workweek
worldwide
worst-case scenario
w-test

Y

yard—see backyard, front yard, pole yard, rail yard, shipyard, scrap yard, switchyard, and wood yard
yearlong (adjective)
year-round (adjective)

Z

-zone (trench-zone data

10.0 COMMONLY MISSPELLED WORDS

absence
abundance
accessible
accidentally
acclaim
accommodate
accomplish
accordion
accumulate
achievement
acquaintance
across
address
advertisement
aggravate
alleged
annual
apparent
appearance
argument
atheist
athletics
attendance
auxiliary
balloon
barbecue
barbiturate
bargain
basically
beggar
beginning
believe
biscuit

bouillon
boundary
Britain
business
calendar
camouflage
cantaloupe
category
cemetery
chagrined
challenge
characteristic
changing
chief
cigarette
climbed
collectible
colonel
colossal
column
coming
committee
commitment
comparative
competent
completely
concede
conceive
condemn
conscientious
consciousness
consistent
continuous

controlled	emperor
coolly	enemy
corollary	entirely
convenient	equipped
correlate	equivalent
correspondence	escape
counselor	especially
courteous	exaggerate
courtesy	exceed
criticize	excellence
deceive	excellent
defendant	exhaust
deferred	existence
dependent	expense
descend	experience
description	experiment
desirable	explanation
despair	extremely
desperate	exuberance
develop	fallacious
development	fallacy
difference	familiar
dilemma	fascinate
dining	feasible
disappearance	February
disappoint	fictitious
disastrous	finally
discipline	financially
disease	forcibly
dispensable	foreign
dissatisfied	forfeit
dominant	formerly
drunkenness	foresee
easily	forty
ecstasy	fourth
efficiency	fulfill
eighth	fundamentally
either	gauge
eligible	generally

genius
government
governor
grievous
guarantee
guerrilla
guidance
handkerchief
happily
harass
height
heinous
hemorrhage
heroes
hesitancy
hindrance
hoarse
hoping
humorous
hypocrisy
hypocrite
ideally
idiosyncrasy
ignorance
imaginary
immediately
implement
incidentally
incredible
independence
independent
indicted
indispensable
inevitable
influential
information
inoculate
insurance
intelligence

intercede
interference
interpret
interrupt
introduce
irrelevant
irresistible
island
jealousy
jewelry
judicial
knowledge
laboratory
legitimate
leisure
length
lenient
license
lieutenant
lightning
likelihood
likely
loneliness
losing
lovely
luxury
magazine
maintain
maintenance
manageable
maneuver
marriage
mathematics
medicine
millennium
millionaire
miniature
minutes
mischievous

missile	parallel
misspelled	parliament
mortgage	particularly
mosquito	pavilion
mosquitoes	peaceable
murmur	peculiar
muscle	penetrate
mysterious	perceive
narrative	performance
naturally	permanent
necessary	permissible
necessity	permitted
neighbor	perseverance
neutron	persistence
ninety	physical
ninth	physician
noticeable	picnicking
nowadays	piece
nuisance	pilgrimage
obedience	pitiful
obstacle	planning
occasion	pleasant
occasionally	portray
occurred	possess
occurrence	possessive
official	potato
omission	potatoes
omit	practically
omitted	prairie
opinion	preference
opponent	preferred
opportunity	prejudice
oppression	preparation
optimism	prescription
ordinarily	prevalent
origin	primitive
outrageous	privilege
overrun	probably
panicky	procedure

proceed
professor
prominent
pronounce
pronunciation
propaganda
psychology
publicly
pursue
quandary
quarantine
questionnaire
quizzes
realistically
realize
really
recede
receipt
receive
recognize
recommend
reference
referred
relevant
relieving
religious
remembrance
reminiscence
repetition
representative
resemblance
reservoir
resistance
restaurant
rheumatism
rhythm
rhythmical
roommate
sacrilegious

sacrifice
safety
salary
satellite
scenery
schedule
secede
secretary
seize
separate
sergeant
several
shepherd
shining
similar
simile
simply
sincerely
skeptic
skeptical
skiing
soliloquy
sophomore
souvenir
specifically
specimen
sponsor
spontaneous
statistics
stopped
strategy
strength
strenuous
stubbornness
subordinate
subtle
succeed
success
succession

sufficient	transferred
supersede	truly
suppress	twelfth
surprise	tyranny
surround	unanimous
susceptible	undoubtedly
suspicious	unnecessary
syllable	until
symmetrical	usage
synonymous	usually
tangible	vacuum
technical	valuable
technique	vengeance
temperature	vigilant
tendency	village
themselves	villain
theories	violence
therefore	visible
thorough	warrant
though	Wednesday
through	weird
till	wherever
tomorrow	wholly
tournament	yacht
tourniquet	yield
tragedy	zoology

11.0 COMMONLY CONFUSED WORDS

Any handbook such as those used in college English courses should suffice to answer most English usage questions. Still, the most common errors are included here for your reference and for clarification. (Sources include *The St. Martin's Handbook* and *The Simon & Schuster Handbook for Writers*, as well as from my own experience editing and teaching.)

a, an. Use "a" with a word that begins with a consonant (a forest), with a sounded h (a hemisphere, a history), or with another consonant sound such as "you" or "wh" (a euphoric moment, a one-sided match, a 1,000-gallon tank). Use "an" with a word that begins with a vowel (an umbrella), with a silent h (an honor), or with a vowel sound (an X-ray). (I often see writers get confused by the "h" rule and write "an history," for example; the test is if it's a sounded h, use "a" not "an.")

accept, except. The verb accept means "receive" or "agree to." *Melanie will accept the job offer.* The preposition except means "aside from" or "excluding." *All the plaintiffs except Mr. Smith decided to accept the settlement offered by the defendant.*

absorption, adsorption. Absorption means to soak up, like a sponge; dissolving in liquid or gas. Adsorption refers to when one entity adheres to another, as in carbon adsorption, where a molecule adheres to the activated carbon surface.

advice, advise. Advice is a noun meaning opinion or suggestion; advise is a verb meaning offer or provide advice. *Jenna advised Sally that Frank's advice was poor.*

affect, effect. Affect is a verb meaning influence or move the emotions of. Effect is a noun meaning result, or, less commonly, a verb meaning bring about. Use the "the" test. If you can put "the" in front of it, you have a noun and effect. *The effect of the rain was a flood.* If "the" can only go after the word, use affect, as in: *The rain affected the roof by causing it to break.*

all ready, already. All ready means fully prepared. Already means previously. We were all ready for Lucy's party when we learned that she had already left.

all right. Always write "all right" as two words.

a lot. A lot is always two words. Avoid in formal (i.e., technical) writing.

a.m., p.m. Use only with numbers, not as substitutes for the words morning, afternoon, or evening.

among, between. Use between for two items or people and among for three or more items or people. *The relationship between the twins is different front that among the other three children.*

amount, number. Use amount for quantities that you cannot count (singular nouns such as water, light, or power). Use number for quantities that you can count (usually plural nouns such as objects or people). *A small number of volunteers cleared a large amount of brush within a few hours.*

and/or. Avoid if possible. Use x, y, or both instead.(I generally try to avoid the slash because it is confusing and seems like lazy writing.)

anion, cation. Anion is an ion with a negative charge; cation is an ion with a positive charge.

any body, anybody, any one, anyone. Note the differences: *Although anyone could enjoy carving wood, not just anybody could make a sculpture like that. Any body of water has its own distinctive ecology. Customers were allowed to buy only two sale items at any one time.*

anyway, anyways. Use anyway, never anyways.

as, because. Avoid using "as" for "because" or when in sentences where its meaning is not clear. For example, does *Carl left town as his father was arriving* mean at the same time as his father was arriving or because his father was arriving?

as, like, such as. For comparisons, use "as" when comparing two qualities that people or objects possess. *The box is as wide as it is long.* Also use "as" to identify equivalent terms in a description. *Gary served as moderator at the town meeting.* Use "like" to indicate similarity but not equivalency: *Hugo, like Jane, was a detailed observer.* In formal writing, "such as" is preferable to "like" in most cases.

assure, ensure, insure. Assure means convince or promise, and its direct object is usually a person or persons. *The candidate assured the voters he would not raise taxes.* Ensure and insure both mean make certain, but insure is usually used in the specialized sense of protection against financial loss. *When the city began water rationing to ensure that the supply would last, the Browns found that they could no longer afford to insure their car wash business.* (Note that some companies avoid using "ensure" as it promises too much: *We will ensure that the site is cleaned up by May 15, 2015.*)

as to. Do not use as to as a substitute for about. *Connie was unsure about* (not as to) *David's intentions.*

because of, due to. Both phrases are used to describe the relationship between a cause and an effect. Use due to when the effect (a noun) is stated first and followed by the verb to be. *His illness was due to malnutrition.* (Illness, a noun, is the effect.) Use because of, not due to, when the effect is a clause, not a noun. *He was sick because of malnutrition.* (He was sick, a clause, is the effect.)

being as, being that. Avoid these expressions (substitutes for because) in formal writing.

beside, besides. Beside, a preposition, means next to. Besides is either a preposition meaning other than or in addition to or an adverb meaning moreover. *No one besides Elaine knows whether the tree is still growing beside the house.*

bi, semi. Bi means every other, and semi means twice in a given period.

breath, breathe. Breath is the noun, and breathe is the verb.

but, yet, however. Use these words separately, not together.

but that, but what. Avoid these as substitutes for that.

can, may. Can refers to ability and may to possibility or permission to do something. *Since I can ski the slalom well, I may win the race. May I leave early to practice?*

can't, couldn't. Avoid all contractions in formal writing.

choose, chose. Choose is the simple form of the verb; chose is the past-tense form. *I chose the movie last week, so you choose it tonight.*

compare to, compare with. Compare to means describe one thing as similar to another. *Juanita compared the noise to the roar of a waterfall.* Compare with is the more general activity of noting similarities and differences between objects or people. *The detective compared the latest photograph with the old one, noting how the man's appearance had changed.*

complement, compliment. Complement means go well with or enhance. Compliment means praise.

comprise, compose. Comprise means contain (the whole comprises the parts). Compose means make up (the parts compose the whole). *The class comprises 20 students. Twenty students compose the class.*

consequently, subsequently. Consequently means as a result or therefore. Subsequently just means afterwards. Roger lost his job, and subsequently I lost mine. Consequently, I was unable to pay my rent.

continual, continuous. Continual describes an activity that is repeated at regular or frequent intervals. Continuous describes either an activity that is ongoing without interruption or an object that is connected without break. *The damage done by continuous erosion was increased by the continual storms.*

couple of. Avoid in formal writing. Say specifically what you mean.

criteria, criterion. Criterion means a standard of judgment or a necessary qualification. Criteria is the plural form.

data. The word data is the plural form of the Latin word datum, meaning a fact or a result collected during research. Treat data as plural in formal writing. *These data indicate that fewer people smoke today than 10 years ago.*

different from, different than. Different from is generally preferred in formal writing.

discreet, discrete. Discreet means tactful or prudent. Discrete means distinct or separate. *The dean's discreet encouragement brought representatives of all the discrete factions to the meeting.*

dispose, dispose of. Dispose means to incline or to be inclined toward something. Dispose of means to throw away.

disinterested, uninterested. Disinterested means unbiased or impartial. Uninterested means not interested or indifferent.

elicit, illicit. The verb elicit means to draw out or evoke. The adjective illicit means illegal.

especially, specially. Especially means very or particularly. Specially means for a special reason or purpose. *The audience especially enjoyed the new composition, specially written for the holiday.*

every day, everyday. Everyday is an adjective used to describe something as ordinary or common. Every day is an adjective modifying a noun, specifying which particular day. I ride the subway every day even though pushing and shoving are everyday occurrences.

every one, everyone. Everyone is an indefinite pronoun; every one is a noun modified by an adjective, referring to each member of a group. Because he began the assignment after everyone else, David knew that he could finish every one of the selections.

explicit, implicit. Explicit means directly or openly expressed. Implicit means indirectly expressed or implied. *The explicit message of the advertisement urged consumers to buy the product while the implicit message promised popularity.*

farther, further. Farther refers to physical distance. *How much farther is it to the jobsite?* Further refers to time or degree. *I want to avoid further delays and further misunderstandings.*

fewer, less. Use fewer with objects or people that can be counted (plural nouns). Use less with amounts that cannot be counted (singular nouns). *The world would be safer with fewer bombs and less* *hostility.*

firstly, secondly, thirdly. These are old-fashioned for introducing a series of points. Use first, second, and third.

following. Following is an adjective (the following items) or a noun (a large following), not a substitute for after. *After the holes were dug*, not *Following the hole digging.*

from . . . to, between . . . and. These have different meanings. *The store operated from 1950 to 1970.* This means the store was open from the year 1950 to the year 1970. *The store operated between 1950 and 1970.* This means the store was open from 1951 to 1969. *Concentrations were detected from 5 mg/kg to 10 mg/kg.* The concentrations, in this case, were from 5 mg/kg to 10 mg/kg. *Concentrations detected were between 5 mg/kg and 100 mg/kg.* In this case, the concentrations were from 6 (or 5.1 . . . anything higher than 5) mg/kg to 99 (or 99.9 . . . anything lower than 100) mg/kg.

good, well. Good is an adjective and should not be used as a substitute for the adverb well. Gabriel is a good host who cooks quite well.

has got to, has to. Avoid these colloquial phrases for must.

have, of. *Have*, not *of*, should follow could, would, should, or might.

he/she, his/her. He/she and his/her are ungainly ways to avoid sexism in writing. Other solutions are to write out *he or she* or to alternate using *he* and *she*. But perhaps the best solution is the eliminate the pronouns entirely or to make the subject plural (they), thereby avoiding all reference to gender. *Everyone should carry his or her driver's license with him or her* could be revised to *Drivers should carry driver's licenses at all times* or to *People should carry their driver's licenses with them.*

hopefully. Hopefully is widely misused to mean it is hoped, but its correct meaning is with hope. Sam watched the roulette wheel hopefully, not Hopefully, Sam will win.

if, whether. Use whether or whether or not (I prefer to just use "whether" without the "or not") to express an alternative. *She was considering whether to buy the new software.* Reserve if for the subjunctive case. *If it should rain tomorrow, our class will meet in the gym.*

impact. As a noun, impact means a forceful collision. As a verb, impact means pack together. *Because they were impacted, Jason's wisdom teeth needed to be removed.* Avoid the colloquial use of impact as a vague word meaning to affect. *Population control may reduce* (not impact) *world hunger.* (Note: I see "impact" used frequently by my clients when "affected" would probably be a better choice such as "the area will not be impacted by construction"; since it is so commonly used and seems to have become acceptable for such use, I often leave as is. Here is a typical example: *To determine the extent of petroleum-hydrocarbon impacted soils in the areas of confirmed impact. . .*
.

imply, infer. To imply is to suggest. To infer is to make an educated guess. Speakers and writers imply; listeners and readers infer. *Beth and Peter's letter implied that they were planning a very small wedding; we inferred that we would not be invited.*

inside, inside of, outside, outside of. Drop of after the prepositions inside and outside. The class regularly met outside the building.

interact with, interface with. Avoid these colloquial expressions.

irregardless, regardless. Regardless is the correct word; irregardless is a double negative.

is when, is where. These vague and faulty shortcuts should be avoided in definitions. *Schizophrenia is a psychotic condition in which* (not when or where) *a person withdraws from reality.*

its, it's. Its is a possessive pronoun, even though it does not have an apostrophe. It's is a contraction for it is; avoid it's and other contractions in formal writing.

lay, lie. Lay means place or put. Its forms are lay, laid, laying, laid, and laid. It generally has a direct object, specifying what has been placed. *She laid her books on the desk.* Lie means recline or be positioned and does not take a direct object. Its forms are lie, lay, lain, lying. *She lay awake until 2 a.m., worrying about the exam.* Funny (and true) story: I was showing a friend of mine how well trained my dog was. I said, "Lay down," and she did not move. My friend said, "Well of course she's not moving; you are using incorrect grammar. You should have said lie down!" He was right, of course. Another incorrect example: In the song "Lay Lady Lay," the phrase "Lay across my big brass bed," should actually be "Lie across my big brass bed."

like, such as. Both like and such as may be used in a statement giving an example or a series of examples. Like means similar to; use "like" when comparing the subject mentioned to the examples. *A hurricane, like a flood or any other major disaster, may strain a region's emergency resources.* Use "such as" when the examples represent a general category of things or people. "Such as" is often used as an alternative to for example. *A destructive hurricane, such as Gilbert in 1988, may drastically alter an area's economy.* Commas are not always necessary before and after the phrase containing such as. *Adding fruits such as apples and pears to the bowl should enhance its appearance.* In technical writing, I often use "e.g." instead of such as or for example: *The majority of residents also depend upon fish and game (e.g., trout, salmon, bear, and moose) obtained through subsistence hunting and fishing activities.*

loose, lose. Lose is a verb meaning misplace. Loose, as an adjective, means not securely attached. *Tighten that loose screw before you lose it.*

lots, lots of. Avoid in formal writing.

may be, maybe. May be is a verb phrase. Maybe, the adverb, means perhaps. *She may be the president today, but maybe she will lose the next election.*

media. Media, the plural form of medium, takes a plural verb. The media are going to cover the council meeting.

Ms. Use Ms. instead of Miss or Mrs. unless a woman specifies another title before her name. Ms. should appear before her first name, not before her husband's name: *Ms. Jane Tate,* not Ms. John Tate.

nor, or. Use "either" with "or" and "neither" with "nor."

off of. Use off rather than off of. The spaghetti slipped off the plate.

on, upon. Upon is old-fashioned; usually, "on" is all you need.

only. When you see the word "only" in a sentence, make sure it is in the correct place. The misplacement of the word "only" can completely change a sentence's meaning. *Emily sang only four songs.* (She could have sang many more, but she did not.) *Emily only sang four songs.* (Did Emily just sing a cappella and not play the songs as well? This is confusing.) *Only Emily sang for the guests.* (Perhaps there were numerous other singers, but they did not sing?) *Emily sang four songs only for the invited guests.* (So staff and uninvited guests could not hear her?)

ordnance, ordinance. Ordnance refers to military supplies such as weapons, ammunition, and combat vehicles. Ordinance refers to a decree or order.

owing to the fact that. Avoid this and other unnecessarily word expressions for because.

percent, percentage. These words identify a number as a fraction of 100. Because they show exact statistics, these terms should not be used casually to mean portion, amount, or number. Generally, the word "percent" is always used with a number while "percentage" is not. *Last year, 70 percent of the dogs at animal control were adopted.* In formal writing, spell out percent rather than using its symbol (%) (However, I often use the % symbol in tables.) Percentage is not used with a specific number. *A large percentage of the population prefers fruit to vegetables.*

precede, proceed. Both are verbs; precede means "come before," and proceed means continue or go forward. *Despite the storm that preceded the campus flooding, we proceeded to class.*

principal, principle. These words are unrelated but are often confused because of their similar spellings. Principal as a noun, refers to a head official or an amount of money loaned or invested. When used as an adjective, principal means most significant. The word meaning a fundamental law, belief, or standard is principle. When Albert was sent to the principal, he defended himself with the principle of free speech. The principal intent of the document was to inform.

raise, rise. Raise means lift or move upward. In the case of children, it means bring up or rear. As a transitive verb, it takes a direct object—someone raises something. *The wedding guests raised their glasses in celebration.* Rise means go upwards. It is not followed by a direct object; something rises by itself. *She saw the steam rise from the kettle and knew the tea was ready.*

respectfully, respectively. Respectfully means with respect. Respectively means in the order given. The brothers, respectively a juggler and an acrobat, respectfully greeted the audience.

set, sit. Set means put or place, and it is followed by a direct object—the thing that is placed. Sit does not take a direct object and refers to the action of taking a seat. *Amelia sat at the picnic table and set her backpack on the ground.*

since. Since has two meanings. The first meaning shows the passage of time (*I have not eaten since Tuesday*); the second and more informal meaning is because (*Since you are in a bad mood, I will go away*). Be careful not to write sentences in which since is ambiguous in meaning. *Since I had knee surgery, I have been doing nothing but watching television.* (Since here could mean either because or ever since. In order to avoid such problems some writers prefer not to use since to mean because.)

some body, somebody, some one, someone. *When somebody comes walking down the hall, I always hope that it is someone I know. In dealing with some body like the senate, arrange to meet consistently some one person who can represent the group.*

stationary, stationery. Stationary is an adjective meaning standing still. Stationery is a noun meaning writing paper or materials. *When the bus was stationary at the train crossing, Karen took out her stationery and wrote a letter.*

than, then. Use the conjunction "than" in comparative statements. *The truck was bigger than my house.* Use the adverb "then" when referring to a sequence of events or emotions. *Jim finished college, and then he went to graduate school.*

that, which. That, always followed by a restrictive clause, singles out the object being described. *The trip that you took to New York was expensive.* Note that the clause after "that" is essential to the meaning; it cannot be deleted. Which may be followed by either a restrictive or a nonrestrictive clause but often is used only with the latter. The which clause may simply add more information about a noun or noun clause, and it is set off by commas. *My house, which is in Palmer, is a two-story duplex.* You can delete the phrase in between the commas and still keep the main idea of the sentence that you want to get across. But you cannot delete the words following *that* without losing the meaning of the sentence. *The book that is on the table is the one I want.*

their, there, they're. "Their" is a pronoun, the possessive form of they. *The clients showed their drawings to the editor.* "There" refers to a place. *There, dinosaurs used to walk.* There also is used with the verb "be" in expletive constructions (there is, there are). *There are three items on the agenda.* (I usually try to edit out "there is" and "there are" as they are unnecessary phrases: *The three items on the agenda are dogs, cats, and elephants.*) They're is a contraction of they are, and, like all contractions, it should be avoided in formal writing.

to, too, two. To is a preposition, generally showing direction or nearness. *Stan drove to Eugene.* Avoid using to after where. *Where are you driving?* (not driving to) Too means also. *I am driving there too.* Two is the number.

toward, towards. Towards is considered archaic; toward is now preferred (per Webster's).

visible, visual. Visible means capable of being seen, while visual means pertaining to sight. *No holes were visible in the tank. The method of examination was visual.*

where. Use where alone, not with prepositions such as at or to. *Where did he drill?* (not drill at)

which, who, that. When referring to ideas or things, use which or that. When referring to people, use who or whom. *My aunt, who was furious, pushed on the door, which was still stuck. The book that I like best is* Old Yeller. *The teacher whom I like best is Ms. Pastorelli. People who are interested can sign up after class.*

Interestingly, animals can be referred to by either who or that, depending on the writer's view of them. Sometimes people refer to pets by using the word who and wild animals by using the word that. *Woody, who is my best friend, is a collie. The wolf that ate the rabbits is now in a pen.*

who, whom. Use who if the following clause begins with a verb. *Monica, who drinks uncontrollably, is my godmother. Monica, who is my godmother, drinks uncontrollably.* Use whom in the following clause, which begins with a pronoun. *I have heard that Monica, whom I have not seen for 10 years, wears only purple.* An exception occurs when a verbal phrase such as *I think* comes between who and the following clause. Ignore such a phrase as you decide which form to use. *Monica, who (I think) wears nothing but purple, is my godmother.* Here is a simple way to remember this rule: Can you replace the word with "she"? If so, use who. Can you replace the word with "her" or "them"? If so, use whom. (The phrase "whom I have not seen" becomes "I have not seen her" as you apply this test.)

who's, whose. Who's is the contraction of who and is. Avoid contractions in formal writing. Whose is possessive. *Whose book is on the counter?*

your, you're. Your shows possession. *Bring your pets to the party.* You're is the contraction of you and are. Avoid contractions in formal writing.

12.0 TERMS AND DEFINITIONS

It is a good idea to create a list of commonly used terms and definitions for your company, so that your list can be added to and pulled from for future documents. It is especially important to have a consistent understanding and definition of a term for all personnel.

The following, for example, are definitions from the FAA Acquisition Management Policy (AMP) (10/2014). Below that are definitions from Title 14, Part 139, Subpart A (as of December 2014).

12.1 FAA AMP Definitions

Access. In general the term "access" is defined as the ability to physically enter or pass through an FAA area or a facility; or having the physical ability or authority to obtain FAA sensitive information, materials and resources. In relation to classified information, the ability, authority or opportunity to obtain knowledge of such information or materials.

Acquisition Executive Board is the primary executive-level body that assists and supports the FAA Acquisition Executive and Joint Resources Council establish, change, communicate, and implement acquisition management policy, practices, procedures, and tools.

Acquisition planning is the process by which all acquisition-related disciplines of an investment program are developed, coordinated, and integrated into a comprehensive plan for executing the program and meeting the stated requirements within the cost and schedule boundaries. Acquisition planning is normally associated with detailed program planning during final investment analysis, but is also important at other times of the lifecycle management process.

Acquisition program baseline establishes the performance to be achieved by an investment program, as well as the cost and schedule boundaries within which the program is authorized to proceed. The acquisition program baseline is a formal document approved by the investment decision authority at the final investment decision, and is a contract between the FAA and the service organization.

Acquisition strategy. The overall concept and approach of an investment program for acquiring a capability to meet the requirements and perform within the boundaries set forth in the acquisition program baseline. The strategy considers all aspects of a program such as acquisition approach, contracting, logistics, testing, systems engineering, risk management, program management, impact on facilities, human factors, schedules, and cost. The results are documented in the implementation strategy and planning document during final investment analysis.

Affiliate business is a business that controls or has the power to control another business, or a third party that controls or has the power to control another business (contractual relationships must be considered).

Agreement with a state government, local government, and/or public authority is a written agreement between the FAA and a state or local government or public authority where the FAA agrees to receive from, or exchange supplies or services with, the other party.

Agreements with private parties are written documents executed by the parties, which call for the exchange of services, equipment, personnel, or facilities, or require the payment of funds to the FAA, or confirm mutual aid and assistance and outline the specific responsibilities of each party. The term includes agreements under which the FAA provides services, equipment, personnel, or facilities and obtains reimbursement on a negotiated basis from the other party. The term excludes procurement contracts for real estate, supplies and services.

Agreements with public entities other than Federal agencies are written documents executed by the parties which call for the exchange of services, equipment, personnel, or facilities, or require the payment of funds to the FAA, or confirm mutual aid and assistance and outline the specific responsibilities of each party. The term includes agreements under which the FAA provides services, equipment, personnel, or facilities and obtains reimbursement on a negotiated basis from the other party.

Alternative dispute resolution (ADR). Any procedure or combination of procedures voluntarily used to resolve issues in controversy without the need to resort to litigation. These procedures may include, but are not limited to, assisted settlement negotiations, conciliation, facilitation, mediation, fact-finding, mini-trials, and arbitration. These procedures may involve the use of neutrals.

Approval. The agreement that an item is complete and suitable for its intended use.

Architect-engineer services are: (1) professional services of an architectural or engineering nature, as defined by State law, if applicable, which are required to be performed or approved by a person licensed, registered, or certified to provide such services; (2) professional services of an architectural or engineering nature performed by contract that are associated with research, planning, development, design, construction, alteration, or repair of real property; and (3) such other professional services of an architectural or engineering nature, or incidental services, which members of the architectural and engineering professions (and individuals in their employ) may logically or justifiably perform, including studies, investigations, surveying and mapping, tests, evaluations, consultations, comprehensive planning, program management, conceptual designs, plans and specifications, value engineering, construction phase services, soils engineering, drawing reviews, preparation of operating and maintenance manuals, and other related services.

Associate program manager for logistics. An integrated logistics support specialist responsible for ensuring that all NAS integrated logistics support requirements are identified and satisfied for each piece of equipment in the lifecycle management process, RE&D program, and major equipment modification program.

Auctioning techniques is a method of screening vendors using commercial competition techniques, and includes such techniques as indicating to an offeror a cost or price that it must meet to obtain further considerations; advising an offeror of its price standing relative to another offeror; and otherwise furnishing information about other offerors' prices. This may only be used for commercially available products.

Baseline. (1) An agreed-to-description of the attributes of a product, at a point in time, which serves as a basis for defining change; (2) an approved and released document, or a set of documents, each of a specific revision; the purpose of which is to provide a defined basis for managing change; (3) the currently approved and released configuration documentation; or (4) a released set of files consisting of a software version and associated configuration documentation.

Best value. A term used during procurement source selection to describe the solution that is the most advantageous to the FAA, based on the evaluation of price and other factors specified by

the FAA. This approach provides the opportunity for trade-offs between price and other specified factors, and does not require that an award be made to either the offeror submitting the highest rated technical solution, or to the offeror submitting the lowest cost/price, although the ultimate award decision may be to either of these offerors.

Budget impact assessment. The process of assessing the budget impact of each alternative solution developed in the investment analysis phase against all existing programs in the FAA's financial baseline for the same years. Standard criteria are used to determine the priority of the candidate program in relation to all others. If the amount of funding available for the years in question is insufficient, offsets from lower priority programs are identified. A budget impact assessment is also performed when considering program baseline changes for existing programs that involve an increase in the cost baseline and the need to reallocate resources.

Business case analysis summarizes the analytical and quantitative information developed during investment analysis in the search for the best means for satisfying mission need. It is the primary information document supporting the initial investment decision.

Cancellation is the termination of the total requirements of all remaining program years of a multi-year contract. Cancellation results when the contracting officer notifies the contractor of nonavailability of funds for contract performance for any subsequent program year, or fails to notify the contractor that funds are available for performance of the succeeding program year requirement.

Cancellation ceiling is the maximum amount that the FAA will pay the contractor which the contractor would have recovered as a part of the unit price, had the contract been completed. The amount, which is actually paid to the contractor upon settlement for unrecovered costs (which

can only be equal to or less than the ceiling), is referred to as the cancellation charge. This ceiling generally includes only nonrecurring costs.

Capability shortfall. The difference between the projected demand for services and the ability to meet that demand with current assets.

Capital Investment Team (CIT). A team composed of representatives from budget and finance, and, as appropriate, representatives of Air Traffic Organization (ATO) vice-presidents and other FAA organizations, responsible for assessments of investment programs to determine whether

the program should be funded. The assessments involve comprehensive reviews based on cost, schedule and performance of the investments. The consolidated budget request is then reviewed and approved by the Joint Resources Council (JRC).

Capital Planning and Investment Control (CPIC). The process used by FAA management to identify, select, control, and evaluate proposed capital investments. The CPIC process encompasses all stages of capital management including planning, budgeting, procurement, deployment, and assessment. Within the FAA, the Acquisition Management System is the CPIC process. Mission analysis and investment analysis are the "select" portion of the CPIC process, solution implementation is the "control" phase, and in-service management is the "evaluate" phase.

Capture Team. Cross-organizational representatives responsible for coordinating integrated decision-making across investment increments necessary to achieve an operational capability for the NAS. Capture teams monitor implementation of each investment increment and may recommend changes in the distribution of financial assets among capability increments to optimize delivery of the operational capability. Capture teams also participate in activities to validate that an operational capability has achieved its projected benefits and to plan and execute remedial action when it has not.

Cardholder means the individual government employee with the organization who is a warranted contracting officer or to whom a written delegation of procurement authority has been issued by the cognizant Chief of the Contraction Office or designee granting the use of purchase and credit transactions made within the established billing period.

Certified cost or pricing data refers to all facts that, at the time of the price agreement, the seller and buyer would reasonably expect to affect price negotiations. The data requires certification, and is factual, not judgmental, and therefore verifiable. While the data do not indicate the accuracy of the prospective contractor's judgment about estimated future costs or projections, they do include the data utilized to form the basis for that judgment. Certified cost or pricing data is more than historical accounting data; it is all the facts that can be reasonably expected to contribute to the soundness of estimates of all future costs and to the validity of determinations of costs already incurred.

Claim, as used herein, means a contract dispute.

Classified information. Official information or material that requires protection in the interest of national security and is classified for such purpose by appropriate classification authority in accordance with the provisions of Executive Orders 12958 "Classified National Security Information," 12968 "Access to Classified Information," and 12829 "National Industrial Security Program."

Commercial component means any component that is a commercial item. The term component means any item supplied to the Federal government as part of an end item or of another component. See **Commercial Item.**

Commercial item can mean any of the following: [Note: For purposes of this document, the term "commercial item" is interchangeable with the terms "commercially available," "commercial component(s)," "commercial product(s)," and "commercial off-the-shelf (COTS)"]:

(A) Any item, other than real property, that is of a type customarily used by the general public or by nongovernmental entities for purposes other than governmental purposes and that has been sold, leased, licensed to the general public; or has been offered for sale, lease, or license to the general public.

(B) Any item that evolved from an item described in paragraph (A) through advances in technology or performance and that is not yet available in the commercial marketplace, but will be available in the commercial marketplace in time to satisfy the delivery requirements under a government solicitation.

(C) Any item that would satisfy a criterion expressed in paragraphs (A) (B) of this definition, but for-(i) modifications of a type customarily available in the commercial marketplace; or (ii) modifications of a type not customarily available in the commercial marketplace made to meet Federal government requirements.

(D) Any combination of items meeting the requirements of paragraphs (A), (B), (C), or (E) of this definition that are of a type customarily combined and sold in combination to the general public.

(E) Installation services, maintenance services, repair services, training services, and other services if such services are procured for support of an item referred to in paragraph (A), (B), (C), or (D) of this definition, and if the source of such services--(i) offers such services to the general public and the Federal government contemporaneously and under similar terms and conditions; and (ii) offers to use the same work force for providing the Federal government with such services as the source uses for providing such services to the general public.

(F) Services of a type offered and sold competitively in substantial quantities in the commercial marketplace based on established catalog or market prices for specific tasks performed under standards commercial terms and conditions. This does not include services that are sold based on hourly rates without an established catalog or market price for specific service performed.

(G) Any item, combination of items, or service referred to in paragraphs (A) through (F), notwithstanding the fact that the item, combination of items, or service is transferred between or among separate divisions, subsidiaries, or affiliates of a contract; or

(H) An item, determined by the procuring agency to have been developed exclusively at private expense and sold in substantial quantities, on a competitive basis, to multiple state and local governments.

Commercial-off-the-shelf is a product or service that has been developed for sale, lease or license to the general public and is currently available at a fair market value. See **Commercial Item.**

Commercial product means a product in regular production that is sold in substantial quantities to the general public and/or industry at established catalog or market prices. See **Commercial Item.**

Commercially available refers to products, commodities, equipment, material, or services available in existing commercial markets in which sources compete primarily on the basis of established catalog/market prices or for which specific costs/prices established within the industry have been determined to be fair and reasonable. See **Commercial Item**.

Commonality refers to the use of identical parts, components, subsystems or systems to achieve economies in development and manufacture.

Communications, when referring to contracting, means any oral or written communication between the FAA and an offeror that involves information essential for understanding and evaluating an offeror's submittal(s), and/or determining the acceptability of an offeror's submittal(s).

Computer resources support. The facilities, hardware, system support software, software/hardware development and support tools (e.g. compilers, PROM burners), documentation, and personnel needed to operate and support embedded computer systems. These items represent the resources required for the operational support engineering functions and do not include administrative computer resources.

Concept development is the second stage in the CMTD process. This activity develops and evaluates promising concepts to determine which should undergo further development. Activities include modeling, simulation, and detailed analysis.

Concept evaluation is the third and final stage in the CMTD process. It confirms that a concept has great promise toward meeting the service needs of the agency and begins to determine operational and technical feasibility. Concept evaluation can include concept integration, evolution, or scalability. Representative activities include prototyping and field demonstration.

Concept exploration is the first stage in the CMTD process. The objective is to describe promising concepts with sufficient definition to begin development of a concept of operations and to plan follow-on activities. Outputs are promising and feasible concepts that warrant further development.

Concept maturity and technology development (CMTD). The CMTD process governs activities directed toward the production of useful materials, devices, systems, and methods, as well as advance the maturity of new concepts. Typical activities include concept feasibility studies, technical analysis, prototype demonstrations, and operational assessments that identify, develop, and evaluate opportunities for improving the delivery of NAS services. These efforts reduce risk, define requirements, demonstrate operational requirements, inform concept and requirements definition activities, and generate information required to support agency investment decisions and product lifecycle management.

Configuration. (1) The performance, functional, and physical attributes of an existing or planned product, or a combination of products; or (2) one of a series of sequentially created variations of a product.

Configuration audit. Product configuration verification

accomplished by inspecting documents, products, and records; and reviewing procedures, processes, and systems of operation to verify that the product has achieved its required attributes (performance requirements and functional constraints), and the product's design is accurately documented. Sometimes divided into separate functional and physical configuration audits.

Configuration change management. (1) A systematic process which ensures that changes to released configuration documentation are properly identified, documented, evaluated for impact, approved by an appropriate level of authority, incorporated, and verified. (2) The configuration management activity concerning the systematic proposal justification, evaluation, coordination and disposition of proposed changes, and the implementation of all approved and released changes into (a) the applicable configurations of a product, (b) associated product information, and (c) supporting and interfacing products and their associated product information.

Configuration documentation. Technical documentation, the primary purpose of which is to identify and define a product's performance, functional, and physical attributes.

Configuration identification. (1) The systematic process of selecting the product attributes, organizing associated information about the attributes, and stating the attributes; (2) unique identifiers for a product and its configuration documents; or (3) the configuration management activity which encompasses selecting configuration documents; assigning and applying unique identifiers to a product, its components, and associated documents; and maintaining document revision relationships to product configurations.

Configuration management. A management process for establishing and maintaining consistency of a product's performance, functional, and physical attributers with its requirements, design, and operational information throughout its life.

Configuration status accounting. The configuration management activity concerning capture and storage of, and access to, configuration information needed to manage products and product information effectively.

Configuration verification. The action verifying that the product has achieved its required attributes (performance requirements and functional constraints) and the product's design is accurately documented.

Contract is a legal instrument used to acquire products and services for the direct benefit or use by the FAA.

Contract. As used herein denotes the document (for example, contract, memorandum of agreement or understanding, purchase order) used to implement an agreement between a customer (buyer) and a seller (supplier).

Contract dispute as used herein, means a written request seeking as a matter of right, the payment of money in a sum certain, the adjustment or interpretation of contract terms, or other relief arising under or relating to the contract. A claim arising under a contract unlike a claim relating to that contract, is a claim that can be resolved under a contract clause that provides for the relief sought by the claimant. The term does not include a request for payment of an invoice, voucher, or similar routine payments expressly authorized under the terms of the contract, which have not been rejected by the contracting officer. The term includes a termination for convenience settlement proposal and request for equitable adjustment, but does not include cost proposals seeking definitization of a letter contract or other undefinitized contract action.

Contractor. The party(ies) receiving a direct procurement contract from the FAA and who is responsible for performance of the contract requirements.

Controversy or concern. A material disagreement between the FAA and an offeror that could result in a protest.

Core policy refers to the official governing policy of the Acquisition Management System. It consists of all Sections and Appendices A-E of this document. All other acquisition information not contained within this policy document is in the form of guidance, processes, references, and other acquisition aids, used by the lifecycle management workforce with discretion and in a manner that makes sense for individual programs. All of this information, including core policy, is considered to be the entire Acquisition Management System. This information may be found within the FAA Acquisition System Toolset on the Internet.

Cost is the contractor's expenses of contract performance, either estimated or actual.

Cost or pricing data. See "Certified Cost or Pricing Data" and "Non-certified Cost or Pricing

Data".

Critical operational issue. A key operational effectiveness or suitability issue that must be examined in operational test and evaluation to determine a product's capability to perform its mission.

Critical performance requirements. Primary requirements of a solution representing attributes or characteristics considered essential to meeting the mission need that the investment program is seeking to satisfy. Critical performance requirements and associated values are specified in the program requirements document.

Customer. External users of FAA products or services, such as airlines and the flying public. See **User.**

Data. Recorded information of any nature (including administrative, managerial, financial, and technical), regardless of medium or characteristics.

Demand, as used in the context of service analysis, is the current or projected demand for FAA products, services, and capacity, based on input from diverse sources such as the aviation community, enterprise architecture, long-range planners, and operators and maintainers of the NAS and other FAA support systems.

Design to cost is a concept that establishes cost elements as management goals to best balance between lifecycle cost, acceptable performance, and schedule. Under this concept, cost is a design constraint during the design, development, and production phases, and a management discipline throughout the system lifecycle.

Direct-work maintenance staffing. The direct person-hours required to operate, maintain, and support a product for the duration of its lifecycle.

Disapproval. Conclusion by the appropriate authority that an item submitted for approval is either not complete or is not suitable or its intended use.

Discriminating criteria/key discriminators, used in procurement context, are those factors expected to be especially important, significant, and critical in the ultimate source selection decision.

Dispute as used herein, means a Contract Dispute or Claim.

Dispute resolution officer is a licensed legal practitioner who is a member of the Office of Dispute Resolution, and who has authority to conduct proceedings, which, if agreed to by the parties and concurred in by the FAA Administrator, result in binding decisions on the parties.

Dominant business is a controlling or major influence in a market in which a number of businesses are primarily engaged. Factors such as business volume; number of employees; financial resources; competitiveness; ownership or control of materials, processes, patents, and license agreements; facilities; sales territory; and nature of the business must be considered.

Economically disadvantaged individuals means disadvantaged individuals whose ability to compete in the free enterprise system is impaired due to diminished opportunities to obtain capital and credit as compared to others in the same line of business who are not disadvantaged.

End product. A system, service, facility, or operational change that is intended for delivery to a customer or end user.

Enterprise architecture products include the operational view family (business rule) and systems view family (engineering). Operational view family components represent a set of graphical and textual products that describe the changes in tasks and activities, operational elements, and information exchanges required to accomplish NAS service delivery or ATO business processes. The business process and application views present this information in the FEAF with the data architecture providing the terms used to describe information exchanges between processes. System view family components represent a set of graphical and textual products that describe systems and interfaces that directly or indirectly support, communicate, or facilitate NAS service delivery or ATO business processes. In the FEAF, interfaces between applications are described in the application view. Also in the FEAF, there is a logical description of systems, but not a physical or geographic description in the enterprise architecture.

Evolutionary product development is the process of establishing a product designed to evolve over time, as opposed to the need for wholesale replacement, to satisfy requirements. The objective is to accommodate rapid insertion of new technology and upgrades, rather than invest in entirely new products.

FAA disputes resolution system is a process established within the FAA for resolving protests of FAA screening information request and contract awards, as well as contract disputes.

FAA Enterprise Architecture (referred to as the enterprise architecture throughout AMS) defines the operational and technical framework for all capital assets of the FAA. It describes the agency's current and target architectures, as well as the transition strategy for moving from the current to the target architecture. The enterprise architecture has two segments: the NAS architecture and the non-NAS architecture. The non-NAS segment uses the Federal Enterprise Architecture Framework (FEAF). The operational view is split between the business process, application, and data views. The systems view in the FEAF is specified in the technical view.

FAA Office of Dispute Resolution for Acquisition is an independent organization within the FAA, reporting to the FAA Chief Counsel, which is staffed with an appropriate number of dispute resolution officers.

Fee is compensation paid to a consultant for professional services rendered.

Firm, as defined for architect-engineering services, is any individual, partnership, corporation, association, or other legal entity permitted by law to practice the professions of architecture or engineering.

Firmware. The combination of a hardware device and computer instructions or computer data that reside as read-only software "burned into" the hardware device; various types of firmware include devices whose software code is erasable/re-programmable to some degree.

First-level technical support. This work comprises maintenance of the National Airspace System infrastructure and includes certifying equipment and performing periodic maintenance, restoration, troubleshooting, and corrective activities.

Functional baseline is the initially approved documentation describing a product's functional, interoperability, and interface characteristics, and the verification required to demonstrate the achievement of those characteristics.

Generic processes. Flowcharts and supporting information, including descriptions, approving officials, references, templates, and other aids that describe each event of a phase of the lifecycle management process. Generic processes are provided to service organizations for guidance to assist in the complex planning, product development, procurement, production, testing, delivery, and implementation activities of this important phase of the lifecycle management process. Generic processes are an integral part of FAST.

Hardware products. Made of material and their components (mechanical, electrical, electronic, hydraulic, pneumatic). Computer software and technical documentation are excluded.

Historically black colleges and universities. Institutions determined by the U.S. Secretary of

Education to meet the requirements of 34 CFR 608.2 and listed therein.

Human factors are a multi-disciplinary effort to generate and apply human performance information to acquire safe, efficient, and effective operational systems.

Implementation strategy and planning is the detailed planning document for all aspects of program implementation. It integrates the planning requirements of several previous FAA planning documents including the program master plan, the integrated logistics support plan, the test and evaluation master plan, the program implementation plan, the human factors plan, and the procurement plan. It is recorded in the implementation strategy and planning document.

In-service decision is the decision to accept a product or service for operational use during the solution implementation phase of the lifecycle management process. This decision allows deployment activities, such as installing products at each site and certifying them for operational use, to start.

In-service management phase of the lifecycle management process, is that period of time after a product or service begins operational use, and continues for as long as the product is in use.

Indian means any person who is a member of any Indian tribe, band, group, pueblo, or community which is recognized by the Federal Government as eligible for services from the Bureau of Indian Affairs in accordance with 25 U.S.C. 1452(c) and any "Native" as defined in the Alaska Native Claims Settlement Act (43 U.S.C. 1601).

Indian organization means any governing body of any Indian tribe or entity established or recognized by the governing body of an Indian tribe for the purposes of 25 U.S.C., chapter 17.

Indian-owned economic enterprise means any Indian-owned (as determined by the Secretary of the Interior) commercial, industrial, or business activity established or organized for the purpose of profit, provided that Indian ownership shall constitute not less than 51 percent of the enterprise.

Indian tribe means any Indian tribe, band, group, pueblo, or community, including native villages and native groups (including corporations organized by Kenai, Juneau, Sitka and Kodiak) as defined in the Alaska Native Claims Settlement Act, which is recognized by the Federal Government as eligible for services from BIA in accordance with 25 U.S.C. 1452 (c).

Integrated logistics support is the functional discipline that plans, establishes, and maintains a full lifecycle support system for FAA products and services. This applies to the sustainment and disposal of fielded products and services as well as new investment programs. The objective is the required level of service to the end user at optimal lifecycle cost to the FAA. The logistics manager is the service-team member who plans, establishes, and maintains an integrated product support package for the lifecycle of FAA products and services.

Interagency agreement is a written agreement between the FAA and another Federal agency where the FAA agrees to receive from, or exchange supplies or services with, the other agency, and FAA funds are obligated.

Interested party. An interested party is one who:

(1) Prior to the close of a solicitation, is an actual or prospective participant in the procurement, excluding prospective subcontractors; or

(2) After the close of a solicitation, is an actual participant who would be

next in line for award under the solicitations scheme if the protest is successful. An actual participant who is not in line for award under the solicitations scheme is ineligible to protest unless that party's complaint alleges specific improper actions or inactions by the agency that caused the party to be other than in line for award. Proposed subcontractors are not eligible to protest.

Where a contract has been awarded prior to the filing of a protest, the awardee may be considered an interested party for purposes of participating in the protest proceedings.

Interface. The performance, functional, and physical attributes required to exist at a common boundary.

Interface control documentation. Interface control drawing or other documentation that depicts physical, functional, and test interface characteristics between two or more related or co- functioning items.

Interim payment is a form of contract financing for cost reimbursement contracts where a contractor is paid periodically during the course of a contract for allowable costs it incurs in the performance of the contract. As interim payments are issued during the course of a contract, they do not include the final payment issued after contract completion.

Intra-agency agreement is a written agreement between the FAA and Office of the Secretary of Transportation or another Department of Transportation operating administration where the requesting organization agrees to provide or exchange supplies or services with the FAA, and FAA funds are obligated.

Investment analysis of the lifecycle management process is conducted to determine the most advantageous solution to an approved mission need. It involves: (1) a market search to determine industry capability, (2) analysis of various alternative approaches for satisfying requirements, (3) and affordability assessment to determine what the FAA can afford, and (4) detailed planning for the alternative selected for implementation.

Investment increment. A discrete activity or investment program that may provide individual benefits and or combine with other investment increments to achieve the benefits of an operational capability.

Investment program. A sponsored, fully funded effort initiated at the final investment decision of the lifecycle management process by the investment decision authority in response to a priority agency need. The goal of an investment program is to field a new capability that satisfies performance, cost, and schedule targets in the acquisition program baseline and benefit targets in the business case analysis report. Typically an investment program is a separate budgeted line-item and may have multiple procurements and several projects, all managed within the single program.

Joint Resources Council is the FAA body responsible for making corporate level decisions.

Lifecycle. The entire spectrum of activity for an FAA capital asset starting with the identification of need and extending through design, development, production or construction, deployment, operational use, sustaining support, and retirement and disposal.

Lifecycle management process. A depiction of the series of phases and decision points that comprise the lifecycle of FAA products and services.

Lifecycle acquisition management system is a fully coordinated set of policies, processes, and computer-based acquisition tools that guide the lifecycle management workforce through the lifecycle management process from the determination of mission needs to the procurement and lifecycle management of products and services that satisfy those needs.

Lifecycle cost is the total cost to the FAA of acquiring, operating, maintaining, supporting, and disposal of systems or services over their useful life. Lifecycle cost includes total investment costs, development costs, and operational costs and includes all appropriations, RE&D, F&E, and OPS.

Line of business. An informal term used to characterize the major organizations of the FAA, headed by the Chief Operating Officer (ATO) or the Assistant or Associate Administrator (non- ATO), having major roles and responsibilities in the lifecycle Acquisition Management System (FAA staff offices led by an Assistant Administrator are considered a line of business for purposes of AMS). They are: Air Traffic Organization; Aviation Safety; Airports; Commercial Space Transportation; Security and Hazardous Materials Safety; Finance and Management; NextGen and Operations Planning; Policy, International, Affairs and Environment; Human Resources; Civil Rights; Government and Industry Affairs; and Communications. See Appendix A for line of business roles and responsibilities.

Maintenance planning. The process is conducted to determine, evolve, and establish hardware and software maintenance concepts and requirements for the lifecycle of a product.

Maintenance support facility. The permanent or semi-permanent real property assets required to support a product. Maintenance support facility management includes conducting studies to define types of facilities or facility improvements, locations, space needs, environmental requirements, real estate requirements and equipment.

Market survey is used in two different contexts in AMS. In terms of the procurement and contracting process, it refers to any method used to survey industry to obtain information and comments and to determine competition, capabilities, and estimate costs. In terms of the lifecycle management process, market surveys are an integral part of investment analysis. After initial requirements are established, market surveys are used as a basis for identifying all potential material and nonmaterial solutions to mission need.

Memorandum of agreement (MOA) is a written document executed by the parties, which creates a legally binding commitment and may require the obligation of funds. However, when the FAA will acquire services, equipment, personnel, or facilities from a contractor for the direct benefit or use of the FAA, a procurement contract should be used.

Memorandum of understanding (MOU) is a written document executed by the parties which establishes policies or procedures of mutual concern. It does not require either party to obligate funds and does not create a legally binding commitment.

Metrics are measurements taken over time that monitor, assess, and communicate vital information about the results of a program or activity. Metrics are generally quantitative, but can be qualitative.

Minority Educational Institutions. Institutions verified by the U.S. Secretary of Education to meet the criteria set forth in 34 CFR 637.4. Also includes Hispanic-serving institutions as defined by 20 U.S.C. 1059c(b)(1).

Mission analysis is that part of the lifecycle management process during which continuous analytical activity is performed to evaluate the capacity of FAA assets to satisfy existing and emerging demands for services. It is conducted within the lines of business organizations of the

FAA.

Multi-year contracts are contracts covering more than one year but not in excess of five years of requirements. Total contract quantities and annual quantities are planned for a particular level and type of funding as displayed in a current five year development plan. Each program year is annually budgeted and funded and, at the time of award, funds need only to have been appropriated for the first year. The contractor is protected against loss resulting from cancellation by contract provisions, which allows reimbursement of costs included in the cancellation ceiling.

Multi-year funding refers to Congressional authorization and appropriation covering more than one fiscal year. The term should not be confused with two-year or three-year funds which cover only one fiscal year's requirement but permit the Executive Branch more than one year to obligate the funds.

NAS enterprise architecture is a NAS-wide enterprise repository of views which describe the current (as-is), mid-term, and far-term (to-be) perspectives of the NAS architecture as well as the strategic planning roadmaps which depict the possible evolution path from the "as is" to the "to be".

NAS technical documentation. Any set of documents that describe the technical requirements of the National Airspace System.

Neutral means an impartial third party, who serves as a mediator, fact finder, or arbitrator, or otherwise functions to assist the parties to resolve the issues in controversy. A neutral person may be a permanent or temporary officer or employee of the federal government or any other individual who is acceptable to the parties. A neutral person shall have no official, financial, or personal conflict of interest with respect to the issues in controversy, unless such interest is fully disclosed in writing to all parties and all parties agree that the neutral person may serve.

NextGen Implementation Plan is an executive-level outline of current activities and program commitments necessary to implement new operational capabilities. The plan is published annually to reflect prior-year accomplishments and new commitments.

No-year funding refers to Congressional funding that does not require obligation in any specific year or years.

Non-certified cost or pricing data is any type of information that is not required to be certified, that is necessary to determine price reasonableness or cost realism. This includes pricing, sales, or cost information, and cost or pricing data for which certification is determined inapplicable after submission.

Non-developmental item (NDI) is an item that has been previously developed for use by federal, state, local, or a foreign government and for which no further development is required.

Non-materiel solution. A solution to an FAA capability shortfall identified during service analysis or investment analysis that is operationally acceptable to users and can be implemented within approved budgets and baselines. Non-materiel solutions typically involve regulatory change, process re-engineering, training, procedural change, or transfer of operational assets between sites.

Nonrecurring costs are those production costs which are generally incurred on a one time basis and include such costs as plant or equipment relocation, plant rearrangement, special tooling and special test equipment, pre-production engineering, initial spoilage and rework, and specialized workforce training.

Operational baseline. The approved technical documentation representing installed operational

hardware and software.

Operational capability. A grouping of operational improvements and operational sustainments to achieve specified service outcomes and benefits.

Operational improvement. A change to operational assets to improve one or more NAS or non- NAS services.

Operational readiness refers to the state of a fielded new system in the NAS. This state is achieved after the system is tested by the FAA at a field test site where it is demonstrated that local site personnel have the ability to fully operate and maintain the new system.

Operational suitability. The capability of a product to be satisfactorily integrated and employed for field use, considering such factors as compatibility, reliability, human performance factors, maintenance and logistics support, safety, and training. The term also refers to the actual degree to which the product satisfies these parameters.

Operational sustainment. A discrete activity to maintain one or more current NAS or non-NAS

services.

Other transaction. Transactions, as referenced in Public Law 104-264, October 9, 1996, which do not fall into the category of procurement contracts, grants, or cooperative agreements.

Owners. Within context of the Air Traffic Organization, owners of the FAA are the President, Congress, flying public, and American taxpayers.

Packaging, handling, storage and transportation. The resources, processes, procedures, design considerations, and methods to ensure that all subsystem, equipment, and support items are preserved, packaged, handled, and transported properly. Included are environmental considerations and equipment preservation requirements for short and long term storage and transportability.

Performance. A quantitative measure characterizing a physical or functional attribute relating to the execution of an operation or function. Performance attributes include quantity (how many or how much), quality (how well), coverage (how much area, how far), timeliness (how responsive, how frequent), and readiness (availability, mission/operational readiness). Performance is an attribute for all systems, people, products and processes including those for development, production, verification, deployment, operations, support, training and disposal. Thus, supportability parameters, manufacturing process variability, reliability and so forth, are all performance measures.

Personnel security. The standards and procedures utilized to determine and document that the employment or retention in employment of an individual will promote the efficiency of the service and is clearly consistent with the interests of the national security.

Portfolio manager. The individual responsible for management and oversight of an investment portfolio designed to achieve specific operational capabilities.

Prescreening. The evaluation of case files for impacts on safety, ATC services, and other intangible benefits, as well as cost/benefits implications, to determine if the proposed change should be implemented.

Price equals cost plus any fee or profit involved in the procurement of a product or service.

Primary engineer or principal consultant is a firm which is held responsible for the overall performance of the services, including that which is accomplished by others under separate or special service contracts.

Procurement strategy meeting is a meeting of organizations with vested interests in the contemplated procurement. The purpose of this meeting is to reach a consensus on the planned course of the acquisition and to obtain the necessary approvals to proceed.

Procurement team means the Contracting Officer, legal counsel, program officials and other supporting staff.

Program requirements document establishes the operational framework and requirements of the line of business with a mission need. It translates mission need into top-level performance, supportability, and benefit requirements that should be satisfied by the fielded capability. It is prepared in the concept and requirements definition phase of the lifecycle management process.

Product baseline is the initially approved documentation describing all of the necessary functional and physical characteristics of the configuration item and the selected functional and physical characteristics designated for production acceptance testing and tests necessary for support of the configuration item. In addition to this documentation, the product baseline of a configuration item may consist of the actual equipment and software.

Product team or service team. A team with a mission, resources, leader, and cross-functional membership, which executes an element of a service organization's mission.

Program decision-making. In general, resource decision-making in the lifecycle management process is at the corporate level and program decision-making is within service organization.

Protest is a written, timely objection submitted by a protester to an FAA screening information request or contract award.

Protester is a prospective offeror whose direct economic interest would be affected by the award or failure to award an FAA contract, or an actual offeror with a reasonable chance to receive award of an FAA contract.

Rational basis. Documented facts that are: (1) objective and verifiable (not unreasonable, capricious or arbitrary), (2) understandable to a reasonable person, and (3) supported by substantial evidence that results in a logical conclusion. The AMS is a tool used to help formulate a rational basis.

Real property is defined as:

(1) Any interest in land, together with the improvements, structures, and fixtures located thereon (including prefabricated movable structures, such as Butler-type storage warehouses and Quonset huts, and house trailers with or without undercarriages), and appurtenances thereto, under the control of any Federal agency, except

   (a) The public domain;

   (b) Lands reserved or dedicated for national forest or national park purposes;

   (c) Minerals in lands or portions of lands withdrawn or reserved from the public domain that the Secretary of the Interior determines are suitable for disposition under the public land mining and mineral leasing laws;

   (d) Lands withdrawn or reserved from the public domain but not including lands or portions of lands so withdrawn or reserved that the Secretary of the Interior, with the concurrence of the Administrator of General Services, determines are not suitable for return to the public domain for disposition under the general public land laws because such lands are substantially changed in character by improvements or otherwise; and

   (e) Crops when designated by such agency for disposition by

severance and removal from the land.

(2) Improvements of any kind, structures, and fixtures under the control of any Federal agency when designated by such agency for disposition without the underlying land (including such as may be located on the public domain, on lands withdrawn or reserved from the public domain, on lands reserved or dedicated for national forest or national park purposes, or on lands that are not owned by the United States) excluding, however, prefabricated movable structures, such as Butler-type storage warehouses and Quonset huts, and house trailers (with or without undercarriages).

(3) Standing timber and embedded gravel, sand, or stone under the control of any Federal agency, whether designated by such agency for disposition with the land or by severance and removal from the land, excluding timber felled, and gravel, sand, or stone excavated by or for the Government prior to disposition.

Record drawings are drawings submitted by a contractor or subcontractor at any tier to show the construction of a particular structure or work as actually completed under the contract.

Recurring costs are production costs that vary with the quantity being produced, such as labor and materials.

Release. The designation by the originating activity that a document or software version is approved by an appropriate authority and is subject to configuration change management procedures.

Requirements. Conditions or capabilities that must be met or exceeded by a product or component to satisfy agency needs. Requirements form the basis for a contract, standard, specification, or other formally imposed document.

Research, engineering and development (RE&D). The RE&D process governs selection and execution of the RE&D portfolio. This portfolio includes systematic studies to gain knowledge or understanding of concepts, products, or procedures that could potentially benefit the aviation community with or without specific application or means by which a specific need may be met such as research related to materials and human factors. These activities inform the NAS enterprise architecture and CMTD activities, but do not lead directly to concept and requirements definition.

Resources. As it applies to contractor personnel security refers to FAA resources including a physical plant, information databases including hardware and software, as well as manual records pertaining to agency mission or personnel.

Screening is the process of evaluating offeror submittals to determine either which offerors/products are qualified to meet a specific type of supply or service, which offerors are most likely to receive award, or which offerors provide the best value to the FAA.

Screening decision is the narrowing of the number of offerors participating in the source selection process to only those offerors most likely to receive award.

Screening information request is any request made by the FAA for documentation, information, or offer for the purpose of screening to determine which offeror provides the best value solution for a particular procurement.

Second-level engineering support. This work comprises engineering support of the National Airspace System infrastructure and includes defining system performance standards, developing and publishing procedures, designing system improvements, and providing support to first-level technical support personnel.

Selection decision is the determination to make an award by the source selection official to the offeror providing the best value to the FAA.

Service-disabled veteran-owned small business is a small business concern that is 51% owned and controlled by a service disabled veteran(s).

Service organization. A service organization is any organization that manages investment resources regardless of appropriation to deliver services. It may be a service unit, program office, or directorate, and may be engaged in air traffic services, safety, security, regulation, certification, operations, commercial space transportation, airport development, or administrative functions.

Simplified purchases are those products or services of any nature that are smaller in dollar value, less complex, shorter term, routine, or are commercially available and are generally purchased on a fixed price basis.

Single-source contracting is to award a contract, without competition, to a single supplier of products or services.

Small business is a business, including its affiliates, that is independently owned and operated and not dominant in producing the products or performing the services being purchased, and one that qualifies as a small business under the federal government's criteria and North American Industry System Classification Codes size standards.

Small business set-aside is the reservation of an acquisition exclusively for participation by small businesses.

Small disadvantaged business means a small business concern that is at least 51 percent unconditionally owned by one or more individuals who are both socially and economically disadvantaged, or a publicly owned business that has at least 51 percent of its stock unconditionally owned by one or more socially and economically disadvantaged individuals and that has its management and daily business controlled by one or more such individuals. This term also means a small business concern that is at least 51 percent unconditionally owned by an economically disadvantaged Indian tribe or Native Hawaiian Organization, or a publicly owned business having at least 51 percent of its stock unconditionally owned by one of these entities which has its management and daily business controlled by members of an economically disadvantaged Indian tribe or Native Hawaiian Organization. The contractor shall presume that socially and economically disadvantaged individuals include Black Americans, Hispanic Americans, Native Americans, Asian-Pacific Americans, Subcontinent Asian Americans, and other minorities or any other individual found to be disadvantaged by the FAA. The contractor shall presume that socially and economically disadvantaged entities also include Indian tribes and Native Hawaiian Organizations.

Small socially and economically disadvantaged business means a small business concern that is at least 51 percent unconditionally owned by one or more individuals who are both socially and economically disadvantaged, or a publicly owned business that has at least 51 percent of its stock unconditionally owned by one or more socially and economically disadvantaged individuals and that has its management and daily business controlled by one or more such individuals. This term also means a small business concern that is at least 51 percent unconditionally owned by an economically disadvantaged Indian tribe or Native Hawaiian Organization, or a publicly owned business having at least 51 percent of its stock unconditionally owned by one of these entities which has its management and daily business controlled by members of an economically disadvantaged Indian tribe or Native Hawaiian Organization. The contractor shall presume that socially and economically disadvantaged individuals include Black Americans, Hispanic Americans, Native Americans, Asian-Pacific Americans, Subcontinent Asian Americans, and other minorities or any other individual found to be disadvantaged by the FAA. The contractor shall presume that socially and economically disadvantaged entities also include Indian tribes and Native Hawaiian Organizations.

Socially disadvantaged individuals - individuals who have been subjected to racial or ethnic prejudice or cultural bias because of their identity as a member of a group without regard to their qualities as individuals.

Solution implementation is the phase of the lifecycle management process that begins after the investment decision authority selects a solution and establishes an investment program. It ends when the new capability goes into service. This phase is led by the service organization assigned by the IDA at the investment decision.

Solution providers. An organization (e.g., service organization or a regional office implementing a construction program) that has the responsibility for providing assets to satisfy National Airspace requirements.

Specification. A document that explicitly states essential technical attributes/requirements for product and procedures to determine that the product's performance meets its requirements/attributes.

Standardization is the practice of acquiring parts, components, subsystems, or systems with common design or functional characteristics to obtain economies in ownership costs.

Strategic sourcing. The collaborative and structured process of critically analyzing an organization's spending and using this information to make business decisions about acquiring products and services more effectively and efficiently.

Supply, as used in the context of mission analysis, is the existing or projected supply of services to its customers, based on information from field organizations that operate and maintain the NAS, from the aviation community, and from the enterprise architecture.

Supply support. All management actions, procedures, and techniques used to determine requirements that acquire, catalog, track, receive, store, transfer, issue, and dispose of items of supply. This includes provisioning for initial support, maintaining asset visibility for financial accountability, and replenishing spares.

Supportability. The degree to which product design and planned logistics resources meet product use requirements.

Support equipment. All equipment (mobile or fixed) required to support maintenance of a product. It includes associated multi-use end items, ground-handling and maintenance equipment, tools, metrology and calibration equipment, test equipment, and automatic test equipment. It includes the procurement of integrated logistics support necessary to maintain the support equipment itself. Operational engineering support systems and facilities are also integral parts of the lifecycle support equipment.

Sustainment. Those activities associated with keeping fielded products operational and maintained. Also applies to the planning, programming and budgeting for fielded products, referred to as sustainment funding.

Technical data. Recorded information regardless of form or character (such as manuals, drawings and operational test procedures) of a scientific or technical nature required to operate and maintain a product over its lifecycle. While computer programs and related software are not technical data, documentation of these programs and related software are technical data. Also excluded is financial data or other information related to contract administration.

Technical leveling is the act of helping an offeror to bring its proposal/offer up to the level of other proposals/offers through successive rounds of communication, such as by pointing out weaknesses resulting from the offeror's lack of diligence, competence, or inventiveness in preparing his proposal.

Technical transfusion is the FAA's disclosure of technical information from one submittal that results in the improvement of another submittal.

Technical opportunity. A technological opportunity exists when a product or capability not currently used in the NAS has the potential to enable the FAA to perform its mission more safely, efficiently or effectively.

Termination for convenience is a procedure that may apply to any FAA contract, including multi-year contracts. As contrasted with cancellation, termination can be effected at any time during the life of the contract (cancellation is effected between fiscal years) and can be for the total quantity or a partial quantity (whereas cancellation must be for all subsequent fiscal year quantities).

Termination liability is the maximum cost the FAA would incur if a contract is terminated. In the case of a multi-year contract terminated before completion of the current fiscal year's deliveries, termination liability would include an amount for both current year termination charges and out year cancellation charges.

Termination liability funding refers to obligating contract funds to cover contractor expenditures plus termination liability, but not the total cost of the completed end items.

Total estimated potential value. The sum of the initial award, unexercised options, the value of any indefinite delivery/indefinite quantity (IDIQ) contract line items (CLINs), estimates for unpriced CLINs, such as preplanned product improvements, estimated value of partially priced items, and any other items the Contracting Officer deems relevant to establishing potential total contract value. The potential contract value should exclude anticipated change orders, pre- planned product improvements which are not established as CLINs, and any other anticipated actions not included in the written contract. Where duplicative or alternative options are established (i.e., if option 1 is exercised, option 2 will not be exercised) the Contracting Officer should include only the value which reflects the highest priced option. For incentive contracts, the maximum liability of the Government should be included in the potential contract value. For IDIQ contracts, the total contract value is the stated maximum amount the total of issued delivery orders cannot exceed.

Training, training support, and personnel skills. The analysis, design, development, implementation, and evaluation of training requirements to operate and maintain the product. This includes: conducting needs analyses; job and task analyses; delivering individual and team training;

resident and nonresident training; on-the-job training; job aids; and logistic support planning for training aids and training installations.

Unauthorized commitment is an agreement entered into by a representative of the FAA who does not have the authority to obligate the FAA to spend appropriated funds.

Unit. One of a quantity of items (products, parts, etc.)

User. Internal FAA user of a product or service, such as air traffic controllers or maintenance technicians.

Validation. Confirmation that an end product or end-product component will fulfill its intended purpose when placed in its intended environment. The methods employed to accomplish validation are applied to selected work products as well as to the end product and end-product components. Work products should be selected on the basis of which are the best predictors of how well the end product and end-product component will satisfy the intended purpose and user needs. Validation may address all aspects of an end product in any of its intended environments, such as operation, training, manufacturing, maintenance, or support services.

Verification. Confirmation that selected work products meet their specified requirements. This includes verification of the end product (system, service, facility, or operational change) and intermediate work products against all applicable requirements. Verification is inherently an incremental process since it occurs throughout the development of the end product and work products - beginning with initial requirements, progressing through subsequent changes, and culminating in verification of the completed end product.

Version. (1) One of several sequentially created configurations of a data product. (2) A supplementary identifier used to distinguish a changed body or set of computer-based data (software) from the previous configuration with the same primary identifier. Version identifiers are usually associated with data (such as files, data bases and software) used by, or maintained in, computers.

Very small business is a business whose size is no greater than 50 percent of the numerical size standard applicable to the North American Industry System Classification Codes assigned to a contracting opportunity.

Work product. A work product in various forms represents, defines, or directs the end product (system, service, facility, or operational change). This can include concepts of operation, processes, plans/procedures, designs/descriptions, requirements/specifications, models/prototypes, contracts/invoices and other documents.

Work breakdown structure. A hierarchical decomposition of the work to be performed to accomplish an approved agency objective. It includes both internal and external work activities and each descending level represents an increasing definition of the work to be performed.

12.2   14 CFR Part 139 Definitions

AFFF means aqueous film forming foam agent.

Air carrier aircraft means an aircraft that is being operated by an air carrier and is categorized as either a large air carrier aircraft if designed for at least 31 passenger seats or a small air carrier aircraft if designed for more than 9 passenger seats but less than 31 passenger seats, as determined by the aircraft type certificate issued by a competent civil aviation authority.

Air carrier operation means the takeoff or landing of an air carrier aircraft and includes the period of time from 15 minutes before until 15 minutes after the takeoff or landing.

Airport means an area of land or other hard surface, excluding water, that is used or intended to be used for the landing and takeoff of aircraft, including any buildings and facilities.

Airport Operating Certificate means a certificate, issued under this part, for operation of a Class I, II, III, or IV airport.

Average daily departures means the average number of scheduled departures per day of air carrier aircraft computed on the basis of the busiest 3 consecutive calendar months of the immediately preceding 12 consecutive calendar months. However, if the average daily departures are expected to increase, then "average daily departures" may be determined by planned rather than current activity, in a manner authorized by the Administrator.

Certificate holder means the holder of an Airport Operating Certificate issued under this part.

Class I airport means an airport certificated to serve scheduled operations of large air carrier aircraft that can also serve unscheduled passenger operations of large air carrier aircraft and/or scheduled operations of small air carrier aircraft.

Class II airport means an airport certificated to serve scheduled operations of small air carrier aircraft and the unscheduled passenger operations of large air carrier aircraft. A Class II airport cannot serve scheduled large air carrier aircraft.

Class III airport means an airport certificated to serve scheduled operations of small air carrier aircraft. A Class III airport cannot serve scheduled or unscheduled large air carrier aircraft.

Class IV airport means an airport certificated to serve unscheduled passenger operations of large air carrier aircraft. A Class IV airport cannot serve scheduled large or small air carrier aircraft.

Clean agent means an electrically nonconducting volatile or gaseous fire extinguishing agent that does not leave a residue upon evaporation and has been shown to provide extinguishing action equivalent to halon 1211 under test protocols of FAA Technical Report DOT/FAA/AR-95/87.

Heliport means an airport, or an area of an airport, used or intended to be used for the landing and takeoff of helicopters.

Index means the type of aircraft rescue and firefighting equipment and quantity of fire extinguishing agent that the certificate holder must provide in accordance with §139.315.

Joint-use airport means an airport owned by the Department of Defense, at which both military and civilian aircraft make shared use of the airfield.

Movement area means the runways, taxiways, and other areas of an airport that are used for taxiing, takeoff, and landing of aircraft, exclusive of loading ramps and aircraft parking areas.

Regional Airports Division Manager means the airports division manager for the FAA region in which the airport is located.

Safety area means a defined area comprised of either a runway or taxiway and the surrounding surfaces that is prepared or suitable for reducing the risk of damage to aircraft in the event of an undershoot, overshoot, or excursion from a runway or the unintentional departure from a taxiway.

Scheduled operation means any common carriage passenger-carrying operation for compensation or hire conducted by an air carrier for which the air carrier or its representatives offers in advance the departure location, departure time, and arrival location. It does not include any operation that is conducted as a supplemental operation under 14 CFR part 121 or public charter operations under 14 CFR part 380.

Shared-use airport means a U.S. Government-owned airport that is co-located with an airport specified under §139.1(a) and at which portions of the movement areas and safety areas are shared by both parties.

Unscheduled operation means any common carriage passenger-carrying operation for compensation or hire, using aircraft designed for at least 31 passenger seats, conducted by an air carrier for which the departure time, departure location, and arrival location are specifically negotiated with the customer or the customer's representative. It includes any passenger-carrying supplemental operation conducted under 14 CFR part 121 and any passenger-carrying public charter operation conducted under 14 CFR part 380.

Wildlife hazard means a potential for a damaging aircraft collision with wildlife on or near an airport. As used in this part, "wildlife" includes feral animals and domestic animals out of the control of their owners.

13.0 ACRONYMS AND ABBREVIATIONS MOST COMMONLY USED AT OUR COMPANY

13.1 Overview

Since this is the first version of our company's style guide, this list of acronyms and abbreviations is a work in progress. Please let the technical editor know of any missing acronyms/abbreviations or of any mistakes in this list. In the meantime, here are some of the acronyms that are currently used in our company's documents, as well as some that might be used in future documents. Again, the most important thing to remember is to be consistent within documents and within the company. Therefore, use this list as a guide for capitalization rules, spelling, and definitions of acronyms. For example, use ArcInfo as presented here instead of ARC/INFO or Arc/Info. *Although all of these forms of ArcInfo have been used in XYZ Company's documents, we have chosen one (based on ESRI's Web site) to use in our documents from now on.*

Note: These are acronyms and abbreviations taken from various company lists and government agency Web site lists; some may not be relevant to your firm, some names may have changed, and your style may be different for others. We suggest that you make notes on your hard copy of which ones to delete, change, or add, as you (or your technical editors) use this document.

If you have purchased our Microsoft Word version of this style guide at our Web site (www.wordsworthwriting.net or www.formsinword.com), you can paste in your own acronym list. We suggest that you paste special, and then select unformatted text, anywhere in the acronym list. Then you can select all the acronyms (the ones here and the new list you have inserted) and choose Table and Sort by paragraph, and you will automatically alphabetize everything. This should save you a lot of time!

Please do let us know (e-mail editor@wordsworthwriting.net) if you see anything that should be changed.

13.2   General Guidelines

General rules for using acronyms and abbreviations follow:

- Always spell out a word or term when it is first used in the text, followed by the acronym or abbreviation in parentheses. You can use the acronym from then on. Examples: The U.S. Environmental Protection Agency (USEPA) and the Alaska Department of Fish and Game (ADF&G) agree that . . .

- It is not necessary to use acronyms. For items appearing only once or twice in a text, it is better to spell them out.

- Standard company style is to include an acronym list at the beginning of each report or proposal. This does not preclude defining each acronym first use, however.

- Please add, delete, and change as you see fit, and turn in your suggestions to the technical editor.

- Certain acronyms and abbreviations are included here that will only be used in figures and tables if needed for spacing, never in the text. Examples include SYST for system.

- Some companies and agencies capitalize all words in their acronyms list, but I do not. I follow the correct capitalization for that term.

13.3   Acronyms & Abbreviations

Sources include client documents (in **bold**) and the FAA, which keeps a current list at *http://www.faa.gov/airports/resources/acronyms/*. Note that I have left the full capitalization used by the FAA for the agency's acronyms although I suggest following normal capitalization rules in your own documents (e.g., kilobits per second, not Kilobits Per Second).

%	use for "percent" only in table/graph/equation
°C	**degrees Celsius (Centigrade)**
°F	**degrees Fahrenheit**

A

A&P	**Airframe and Powerplant**
A/C	Aircraft
A/G	Air to Ground

A/H	Altitude/Height
AAC	Mike Monroney Aeronautical Center
AAF	Army Air Field
AAI	Arrival Aircraft Interval
AAP	Advanced Automation Program
AAR	Airport Acceptance Rate
ABDIS	Automated Data Interchange System Service B
AC	Advisory Circular
AC	**alternating current**
ACAIS	Air Carrier Activity Information System
ACAS	Aircraft Collision Avoidance System
ACC	Airports Consultants Council
ACC	Area Control Center
ACCT	Accounting Records
ACD	Automatic Call Distributor
ACDO	Air Carrier District Office
ACF	Area Control Facility
ACFO	Aircraft Certification Field Office
ACFT	Aircraft
ACID	Aircraft Identification
ACI-NA	Airports Council International - North America
ACIP	Airport Capital Improvement Plan
ACK	**acknowledgement (message)**
ACLS	Automatic Carrier Landing System
ACLT	Actual Landing Time Calculated
ACM	**Additional Crew Member**
ACO	Aircraft Certification Office
ACO	Office of Airports Compliance and Field Operations
ACP	**Audio Control Panel**
ACRP	Airport Cooperative Research Program
ACT	**altitude compensation tilt**
ACU	**Aircraft Communications Unit**
ADA	Air Defense Area
ADAP	Airport Development Aid Program
ADAS	AWOS Data Acquisition System
ADC	**air data computer**
ADCCP	Advanced Data Communications Control Procedure

ADDA	Administrative Data
ADDS	**Airborne Dispersant Delivery System**
ADF	**Automatic Direction Finder**
ADF	Automatic Direction Finding
ADG	Airplane Design Group
ADI	**attitude director indicator**
ADI	Automatic De-Ice and Inhibitor
ADIN	AUTODIN Service
ADIZ	Air Defense Identification Zone
ADJ	**adjustment**
ADL	Aeronautical Data-Link
ADLY	Arrival Delay
ADO	Airline Dispatch Office
ADP	Automated Data Processing
ADS	Automatic Dependent Surveillance
ADS-B	Automatic Dependent Surveillance-Broadcast
ADSIM	Airfield Delay Simulation Model
ADSY	Administrative Equipment Systems
ADTN	Administrative Data Transmission Network
ADTN2000	Administrative Data Transmission Network 2000
ADVO	Administrative Voice
AED	**automated external defibrillator**
AEG	Aircraft Evaluation Group
AERA	Automated En-Route Air Traffic Control
AEX	Automated Execution
AF	Airway Facilities
AFB	Air Force Base
AFIS	Automated Flight Inspection System
AFM	**Airplane Flight Manual**
AFP	Area Flight Plan
AFRES	Air Force Reserve Station
AFS	**Air Force Station**
AFS	Airways Facilities Sector
AFSFO	AFS Field Office
AFSFU	AFS Field Unit
AFSOU	AFS Field Office Unit (Standard is AFSFOU)
AFSS	Automated Flight Service Station

AFTN	Automated Fixed Telecommunications Network
AGIS	Airports Geographic Information System
AGL	Above Ground Level
AID	Airport Information Desk
AIG	Airbus Industries Group
AIM	**Aeronautical Information Manual**
AIM	Airman's Information Manual
AIP	**Aeronautical Information Publication**
AIP	Airport Improvement Plan
AIR COND	**air conditioning**
AIRMET	Airmen's Meteorological Information
AIRNET	Airport Network Simulation Model
AIS	Aeronautical Information Service
AIT	Automated Information Transfer
AIU	**Audio Interface Unit**
ALP	Airport Layout Plan
ALS	Approach Lighting System
ALSF1	ALS with Sequenced Flashers I
ALSF2	ALS with Sequenced Flashers II
ALSIP	Approach Lighting System Improvement Plan
ALT	**altitude**
ALTRV	Altitude Reservation
AMASS	Airport Movement Area Safety System
AMC	**Air Mobility Command**
AMCC	ACF/ARTCC Maintenance Control Center
AMM	**airplane maintenance mode**
AMOS	Automated Meteorological Observation Station
AMP	ARINC Message Processor (OR) Airport Master Plan
Amps	**amperes**
AMVER	Automated Mutual Assistance Vessel Rescue System
ANC	Alternate Network Connectivity
ANCA	Airport Noise and Capacity Act
ANG	Air National Guard
ANGB	Air National Guard Base
ANMS	Automated Network Monitoring System
ANSI	American National Standards Group
ANT	**Antenna**

AOA	Air Operations Area
AOM	**Airplane Operations Manual**
AP	Acquisition Plan
AP	**autopilot**
APD	**Aircrew Program Designee**
APM	**Aircrew Program Manager**
APP	Approach
APPR/APRCH	**approach**
APS	Airport Planning Standard
APU	**auxiliary power unit**
AQAFO	Aeronautical Quality Assurance Field Office
ARAC	Army Radar Approach Control (AAF)
ARAC	Aviation Rulemaking Advisory Committee
ARC	Airport Reference Code
ARCTR	FAA Aeronautical Center or Academy
ARF	Airport Reservation Function
ARFF	Aircraft Rescue and Fire Fighting
ARINC	Aeronautical Radio, Inc.
ARLNO	Airline Office
ARO	Airport Reservation Office
ARP	Aerospace Recommended Practice
ARP	Airport Reference Point
ARRA	American Recovery and Reinvestment Act of 2009
ARSA	Airport Service Radar Area
ARSR	Air Route Surveillance Radar
ARTCC	Air Route Traffic Control Center
ARTS	Automated Radar Terminal System
ASAS	Aviation Safety Analysis System
ASC	AUTODIN Switching Center
ASCP	Aviation System Capacity Plan
ASD	Aircraft Situation Display
ASDA	Accelerate Stop Distance Available
ASEL	**altitude preselect**
ASLAR	Aircraft Surge Launch And Recovery
ASM	Available Seat Mile
ASOS	Automatic Surface Observation System
ASP	Arrival Sequencing Program

ASQP	Airline Service Quality Performance
ASR	Airport Surveillance Radar
ASTA	Airport Surface Traffic Automation
ASV	Airline Schedule Vendor
ASV	Annual Service Volume
AT	Air Traffic
ATA	Air Transport Association of America
ATAS	Airspace and Traffic Advisory Service
ATC	Air Traffic Control
ATCAA	Air Traffic Control Assigned Airspace
ATCBI	Air Traffic Control Beacon Indicator
ATCCC	Air Traffic Control Command Center
ATCO	Air Taxi Commercial Operator
ATCRB	Air Traffic Control Radar Beacon
ATCRBS	Air Traffic Control Radar Beacon System
ATCSCC	Air Traffic Control Systems Command Center
ATCT	Airport Traffic Control Tower
ATIS	Automated Terminal Information Service
ATISR	ATIS Recorder
ATM	Air Traffic Management
ATM	**Air Turbine Motor**
ATM	Asynchronous Transfer Mode
ATMS	Advanced Traffic Management System
ATN	Aeronautical Telecommunications Network
ATODN	AUTODIN Terminal (FUS)
ATOMS	Air Traffic Operations Management System
ATOVN	AUOTVON (Facility)
ATP	**Airline Transport Pilot**
ATS	Air Traffic Service
ATSCCP	ATS Contingency Command Post
ATT	**attitude**
AUTO	**automatic**
AUTODIN	DoD Automatic Digital Network
AUTOVON	DoD Automatic Voice Network
AUX	**auxiliary**
AV	**Aviation**

AVN	Aviation Standards National Field Office, Oklahoma City
AVON	AUTOVON Service
AWIS	Airport Weather Information
AWOS	Automated Weather Observation System
AWP	Aviation Weather Processor
AWPG	Aviation Weather Products Generator
AWS	Air Weather Station

B

BANS	BRITE Alphanumeric System
BARO	**barometric**
BART	Billing Analysis Reporting Tool (GSA software tool)
BASIC	Basic Contract Observing Station
BASOP	Military Base Operations
BATT	**battery**
BC	**back course**
BCA	Benefit/Cost Analysis
BCR	Benefit/Cost Ratio
BDAT	Digitized Beacon Data
BFO	**beat frequency oscillator**
BIT	**built-in test**
BITE	**built-in test equipment**
BMP	Best Management Practices
BOC	Bell Operating Company
BOW	**Basic Operating Weight**
bps	bits per second
BRG	**bearing**
BRI	Basic Rate Interface
BRITE	Bright Radar Indicator Terminal Equipment
BRL	Building Restriction Line
BRT	**bright**
BUEC	Back-up Emergency Communications
BUECE	Back-up Emergency Communications Equipment

C

C	**Captain**

C/S/S/N	Capacity/Safety/Security/Noise
CAA	Civil Aviation Authority
CAA	Clean Air Act
CAB	Civil Aeronautics Board
CAC	Citizen's Advisory Committee
CAD	Computer Aided Design
CAR	**Civil Air Regulations**
CARF	Central Altitude Reservation Facility
CASFO	Civil Aviation Security Office
CASS	**Cockpit Access Security System**
CAT	Category
CAT	Clear Air Turbulence
CAU	Crypto Ancillary Unit
CB	**bromochloromethane**
CBI	Computer Based Instruction
CBP	**U.S. Customs and Border Protection**
CC&O	Customer Cost and Obligation
CCC	Communications Command Center
CCCC	Staff Communications
CCCH	Central Computer Complex Host
CCS7 -NI	Communication Channel Signal-7 Network Interconnect
CCSD	Command Communications Service Designator
CCU	Central Control Unit
CD	Common Digitizer
CDH	**Control Display Head**
CDI	**Course Deviation Indicator**
CDI	**course deviation indicator**
CDL	**Configuration Deviation List**
CDR	Cost Detail Report
CDS	**Control Display System**
CDS/R	**Control Display System/Retrofit**
CDT	Controlled Departure Time
CDTI	Cockpit Display of Traffic Information
CDU	**Control Display Unit**
CENTX	Central Telephone Exchange
CEP	Capacity Enhancement Program

CEPAC	**Central East Pacific**
CEQ	Council on Environmental Quality
CERAP	Center Radar Approach Control
CERAP	Central Radar Approach
CERAP	Combined Center/Radar Approach Control
CFC	Central Flow Control
CFCF	Central Flow Control Facility
CFCS	Central Flow Control Service
CFR	Code of Federal Regulations
CFWP	Central Flow Weather Processor
CFWU	Central Flow Weather Unit
CG	**center of gravity**
CGAS	Coast Guard Air Station
CGS	**Coast Guard Station**
CHK	**check**
CIP	Capital Improvement Plan
CLC	Course Line Computer
CLIN	Contract Line Item
CLR	**clear**
CLT	Calculated Landing Time
CM	Commercial Service Airport
CNMPS	Canadian Minimum Navigation Performance Specification Airspace
CNS	Consolidated NOTAM System
CNSP	Consolidated NOTAM System Processor
CO	Central Office
CO^2	**carbon dioxide**
COE	U.S. Army Corps of Engineers
COINS	**Commercial Operations Integrated System**
COM	**communications**
COMAT	**Company Material**
COMCO	Command Communications Outlet
COMPT	**compartment**
CONT	**control**
CONUS	Continental United States
COO	**Chief Operating Officer**
CORP	Private Corporation other than ARINC or MITRE

CPA	**closest point of approach**
CPE	Customer Premise Equipment
CPLD	**coupled**
CPMIS	Consolidated Personnel Management Information System
CPR	**cardiopulmonary resuscitation**
CRA	Conflict Resolution Advisory
CRAF	**Civil Reserve Airfleet**
CRDA	Converging Runway Display Aid
CRM	**Crew Resource Management**
CRS	**course**
CRT	Cathode Ray Tube
CSA	Communications Service Authorization
CSIS	Centralized Storm Information System
CSO	Customer Service Office
CSR	Communications Service Request
CSS	Central Site System
CTA	Control Area
CTA	Controlled Time of Arrival
CTA/FIR	Control Area/Flight Information Region
CTAF	Common Traffic Advisory Frequency
CTAS	Center Tracon Automation System
CTL	**control**
CTMA	Center Traffic Management Advisor
CUPS	Consolidated Uniform Payroll System
CVFR	Controlled Visual Flight Rules
CVTS	Compressed Video Transmission Service
CW	Continuous Wave
CWA	Clean Water Act
CWSU	Central Weather Service Unit
CWY	Clearway

D

DA	Decision Altitude/Decision Height
DA	Descent Advisor
DA	Direct Access
DABBS	DITCO Automated Bulletin Board System

DAIR	Direct Altitude and Identity Readout
DAR	Designated Agency Representative
DARC	Direct Access Radar Channel
dB	**decibel**
dBA	Decibels A-weighted
DBCRC	Defense Base Closure and Realignment Commission
DBE	Disadvantaged Business Enterprise
DBMS	Data Base Management System
DBRITE	Digital Bright Radar Indicator Tower Equipment
DC	**direct current**
DCA	Defense Communications Agency
DCAA	Dual Call, Automatic Answer Device
DCCU	Data Communications Control Unit
DCE	Data Communications Equipment
DDA	Dedicated Digital Access
DDD	Direct Distance Dialing
DDM	Difference in Depth of Modulation
DDPG	**Dispatch Deviation Procedures Guide**
DDS	Digital Data Service
DEA	Drug Enforcement Agency
DEC	**decrease**
DEDS	Data Entry and Display System
DEG	**degree(s)**
DEGRAD	**degrade**
DEIS	Draft Environmental Impact Statement
DEL	**delete**
DEP	Departure
DEST	**destination**
DET	**detector**
DEV	**device (deviation)**
DEWIZ	Distance Early Warning Identification Zone
DF	Direction Finder
DFAX	Digital Facsimile
DFDR	**Digital Flight Data Recorder**
DFI	Direction Finding Indicator
DG	**directional gyro**
DGPS	Differential Global Positioning Satellite (System)

DGRAD	**degrade**
DH	Decision Height
DID	Direct Inward Dial
DIFF	**differential**
DIM	**dimming**
DIP	Drop and Insert Point
DIR	**direct**
DIRF	Direction Finding
DISENG	**disengage**
DITCO	Defense Information Technology Contracting Office Agency
DL	**data loader**
DME	Distance Measuring Equipment
DME/P	Precision Distance Measuring Equipment
DMI	**Deferred Maintenance Item**
DMN	Data Multiplexing Network
DN	**down**
DNL	Day-Night Equivalent Sound Level (Also called Ldn)
DoD	U.S. Department of Defense
DOD	Direct Outward Dial
DOI	U.S. Department of Interior
DOS	U.S. Department of State
DOT	U.S. Department of Transportation
DOTCC	U.S. Department of Transportation Computer Center
DOTS	Dynamic Ocean Tracking System
DR	**dead reckoning**
DSCS	Digital Satellite Compression Service
DSPY	**display**
DSUA	Dynamic Special Use Airspace
DTS	Dedicated Transmission Service
DU	**Display Unit**
DUAT	Direct User Access Terminal
DVFR	Day Visual Flight Rules
DVFR	Defense Visual Flight Rules
DVOR	Doppler Very High Frequency Omni-Directional Range
DYSIM	Dynamic Simulator

E

E	**east**
EA	Environmental Assessment
EARTS	En Route Automated Radar Tracking System
ECOM	En Route Communications
ECVFP	Expanded Charted Visual Flight Procedures
EDCT	Expedite Departure Path
EEPROM	**electrically erasable programmable read-only memory**
EFAS	En Route Flight Advisory Service
EFC	Expect Further Clearance
EFIS	Electronic Flight Information Systems
EFIS	**Electronic Flight Instrument System**
EGPWS	**Enhanced Ground Proximity Warning System**
EGT	**exhaust gas temperature**
EIAF	Expanded Inward Access Features
EIS	Environmental Impact Statement
ELEV	**elevator**
ELT	Emergency Locator Transmitter
ELWRT	Electrowriter
EMAS	Engineered Materials Arresting System
EMER	**emergency**
EMI	**electromagnetic interference**
EMPS	En Route Maintenance Processor System
EMS	Environmental Management System
E-MSAW	En-Route Automated Minimum Safe Altitude Warning
ENAV	En Route Navigational Aids
ENG	**engine**
ENT	**enter**
EOBT	**Estimate Off Block Time**
EOF	Emergency Operating Facility
EPA	Environmental Protection Agency
EPIRB	**Emergency Position Indicating Radio Beacon**
EPS	Engineered Performance Standards
EPSS	Enhanced Packet Switched Service
ERAD	En Route Broadband Radar

ERR	**error**
ESC	**escape**
ESEC	En Route Broadband Secondary Radar
ESF	Extended Superframe Format
ESIS	**Electronic Standby Instrument System**
ESP	En Route Spacing Program
ESS	**essential**
ESYS	En Route Equipment Systems
ET	**elapsed time**
ETA	Estimated Time of Arrival
ETD	**Estimated Time of Departure**
ETE	Estimated Time En Route
ETG	Enhanced Target Generator
ETMS	Enhanced Traffic Management System
ETN	Electronic Telecommunications Network
ETP	**Equal Time Point**
EVAC	**evacuate/evacuation**
EVAS	Enhanced Vortex Advisory System
EVCS	Emergency Voice Communications System
EXT	**external/extend**

F

F&E	Facilities and Equipment
FAA	Federal Aviation Administration
FAAAC	FAA Aeronautical Center
FAACIS	FAA Communications Information System
FAATC	FAA Technical Center
FAATSAT	FAA Telecommunications Satellite
FAC	Facility
FAF	Final Approach Fix
FAF	**final approach fix**
FAP	Final Approach Point
FAPM	FTS2000 Associate Program Manager
FAR	Federal Aviation Regulation
FAST	Final Approach Spacing Tool
FATO	Final Approach and Take Off
FAX	Facsimile Equipment

FBO	Fixed Base Operator
FBS	Fall Back Switch
FC	**Flight Crew**
FCC	Federal Communications Commission
FCLT	Freeze Calculated Landing Time
FCOM	FSS Radio Voice Communications
FCPU	Facility Central Processing Unit
FCS	**Flight Control System**
FDAT	Flight Data Entry and Printout (FDEP) and Flight Data Service
FDE	Flight Data Entry
FDEP	Flight Data Entry and Printout
FDIO	Flight Data Input/Output
FDIOC	Flight Data Input/Output Center
FDIOR	Flight Data Input/Output Remote
FDM	Frequency Division Multiplexing
FDP	Flight Data Processing
FDR	**flight data recorder**
FE	**Flight Engineer**
FED	Federal
FEIS	Final Environmental Impact Statement
FEP	Front End Processor
FF	**fuel flow**
FFAC	From Facility
FGS	**Flight Guidance System**
FIFO	Flight Inspection Field Office
FIG	Flight Inspection Group
FIL/FILT	**filter**
FINO	Flight Inspection National Field Office
FIPS	Federal Information Publication Standard
FIR	Flight Information Region
FIRE	Fire Station
FIRMR	Federal Information Resource Management Regulation
FL	Flight Level
FLOWSIM	Traffic Flow Planning Simulation
FLP	**flap**

FLT	**flight**
FMA	Final Monitor Aid
FMF	Facility Master File
FMIS	FTS2000 Management Information System
FMS	Flight Management System
FN	**function**
FNMS	FTS2000 Network Management System
FO	**First Officer**
FOD	**foreign object damage**
FOIA	Freedom of Information Act
FOM	**Figure of Merit**
FONSI	Finding of No Significant Impact
FOS	**Flight Operations System**
FP	Flight Plan
FPD	**freezing point depressant**
FPM	**feet per minute**
FRC	Request Full Route Clearance
FREQ	**frequency**
FSAS	Flight Service Automation System
FSBY	**forced standby**
FSDO	Flight Standards District Office
FSDPS	Flight Service Data Processing System
FSEP	Facility/Service/Equipment Profile
FSO	**Facility Security Officer**
FSP	Flight Strip Printer
FSPD	Freeze Speed Parameter
FSS	Flight Service Station
FSSA	Flight Service Station Automated Service
FSTS	Federal Secure Telephone Service
FSYS	Flight Service Station Equipment Systems
FT	**flight time**
FT	**foot/feet**
FT-LB	**foot-pound**
FTS	Federal Telecommunications System
FTS2000	Federal Telecommunications System 2000
FUS	Functional Units or Systems
FWCS	Flight Watch Control Station

FWD	**forward**

G

G	**gravity**
G/A	**go-around**
G/S	**glideslope**
GA	General Aviation
GAA	General Aviation Activity
GAAA	General Aviation Activity and Avionics
GADO	General Aviation District Office
GAL	**gallon**
GCA	Ground Control Approach
GCA	**ground controlled approach**
GEN	**generator**
GIS	Geographic Information System
GMAP	**ground mapping**
GMM	**General Maintenance Manual**
GMT	**Greenwich Mean Time**
GNAS	General National Airspace System
GND	**GND**
GNSS	Global Navigation Satellite System
GOES	Geostationary Operational Environmental Satellite
GOESF	GOES Feed Point
GOEST	GOES Terminal Equipment
GOM	**General Operations Manual**
GOV	**governor/governing**
GPRA	Government Performance Results Act
GPS	Global Positioning System
GPU	**ground power unit**
GPWS	Ground Proximity Warning System
GRADE	Graphical Airspace Design Environment
GRD	**ground**
GS	Glide Slope Indicator
GSA	General Services Administration
GSE	Ground Support Equipment
GSPD	**groundspeed**
GTC	**gas turbine compressor**

H

H	Non-Directional Radio Homing Beacon (NDB)
HAA	Height Above Airport
HAL	Height Above Landing
HARS	High Altitude Route System
HAT	Height Above Touchdown
HAZMAT	Hazardous Material
HCAP	High Capacity Carriers
HDG	**heading**
HDME	NDB with Distance Measuring Equipment
HDQ	FAA Headquarters
HELI	Heliport
HF	High Frequency
Hg	**Mercury**
HH	NDB, 2kw or More
HI-EFAS	High Altitude EFAS
HI	**high**
HLD	**hold**
HLDC	High Level Data Link Control
HM	**hazardous materials**
HMR	**Hazardous Material Regulations**
HOV	High Occupancy Vehicle
HPa	**hecto-pascal**
HPZ	Heliport Protection Zone
HSI	Horizontal Situation Indicators
HUD	Housing and Urban Development
HVOX	**headphone VOX**
HWAS	Hazardous In-Flight Weather Advisory
HYD	**hydraulic**
Hz	**hertz (Note: FAA defines as HERTZ)**

I

I/AFSS	International AFSS
IA	Indirect Access
IAF	Initial Approach Fix
IAP	Instrument Approach Procedures
IAPA	Instrument Approach Procedures Automation

IAS	**indicated airspeed**
IBM	International Business Machines
IBP	International Boundary Point
IBR	Intermediate Bit Rate
ICAO	International Civil Aviation Organization
ICP	**Intercom Control Panel**
ICS	**Interphone Communication System**
ICSS	International Communications Switching Systems
IDAT	Interfacility Data
IDENT	**identify/identification**
IF	Intermediate Fix
IFCP	Interfacility Communications Processor
IFDS	Interfacility Data System
IFEA	In-Flight Emergency Assistance
IFO	International Field Office
IFR	Instrument Flight Rules
IFSS	International Flight Service Station
ILS	Instrument Landing System
IM	Inner Marker
IMC	Instrument Meteorological Conditions
in. lb.	**inch-pound**
IN.	**inch**
INCR	**increase**
IND	**indicator**
INFO	**Information for Operators**
inHg	**inches of mercury**
INIT	**initialize/initialization**
INM	Integrated Noise Model
INS	Inertial Navigation System
INSP LT	**inspection light**
INST	**instrument**
INTMED	**intermediate**
INTPH	**interphone**
INV	**inverter**
IOE	**Initial Operating Experience**
IRMP	Information Resources Management Plan
IRS	**Inertial Reference System**
IRU	**inertial reference unit**

ISA	**International Standard Atmosphere**
ISDN	Integrated Services Digital Network
ISMLS	Interim Standard Microwave Landing System
ISOL	**isolated**
ITI	Interactive Terminal Interface
IVRS	Interim Voice Response System
IW	Inside Wiring

K

Kbps	Kilobits Per Second
KCAS	**knots calibrated airspeed**
Khz	Kilohertz
KIAS	**knots indicated airspeed**
KTAS	**knots true airspeed**
KTS	**knots**
kVA	**kilovolt-ampere**
KVDT	Keyboard Video Display Terminal

L

L	**left**
LAA	Local Airport Advisory
LAAS	Low Altitude Alert System
LABS	Leased A B Service
LABSC	LABS GS-200 Computer
LABSR	LABS Remote Equipment
LABSW	LABS Switch System
LAHSO	Land and Hold Short Operation
LAN	Local Area Network
LAT	**latitude**
LATA	Local Access and Transport Area
LAWRS	Limited Aviation Weather Reporting System
lb.	**pound**
LBA	Load-Bearing Area
LCD	**liquid crystal display**
LCF	Local Control Facility
LCN	Local Communications Network
LDA	Landing Directional Aid

LDA	Localizer Directional Aid
LDIN	Lead-in Lights
LEC	Local Exchange Carrier
LED	**light-emitting diode**
LF	Low Frequency
LH	**left hand**
LINCS	Leased Interfacility NAS Communications System
LIS	Logistics and Inventory System
LLWAS	Low Level Wind Shear Alert System
LM	**Loadmaster**
LM/MS	Low/Medium Frequency
LMM	Locator Middle Marker
LMS	LORAN Monitor Site
LNAV	**lateral navigation**
LO	**low**
LOC	**localizer**
LOC	Localizer
LOCID	Location Identifier
LOI	Letter of Intent
LOM	Compass Locator at Outer Marker
LOM	**locator outer marker**
LONG	**longitude**
LORAN	Long Range Aid to Navigation
LPV	Lateral Precision Performance with Vertical Guidance
LRCO	Limited Remote Communications Outlet
LRNAV	Long Range Navigation
LRR	Long Range Radar
LSGI	**low-speed ground idle**
LSR	**low speed range**
LT	**light or local time**

M

MAA	Maximum Authorized Altitude
MAC	**mean aerodynamic chord**
MAG	**magnetic**
MAINT	**maintenance**
MALS	Medium Intensity Approach Lighting System

MALSF	MALS with Sequenced Flashers
MALSR	MALS with Runway Alignment Indicator Lights
MAN	**manual**
MANF	**manifold**
MAP	Maintenance Automation Program
MAP	Military Airport Program
MAP	Missed Approach Point
MAP	Modified Access Pricing
MAX	**maximum**
MB	**millibar**
Mbps	Megabits Per Second
MCA	Minimum Crossing Altitude
MCAS	Marine Corps Air Station
MCC	Maintenance Control Center
MCL	Middle Compass Locater
MCS	Maintenance and Control System
MDA	Minimum Descent Altitude
MDH	**minimum descent height**
MDT	Maintenance Data Terminal
MEA	Minimum En Route Altitude
MECH	**mechanical**
MEL	**Minimum Equipment List**
METI	Meteorological Information
MF	Middle Frequency
MFD	**Multifunction Display**
MFJ	Modified Final Judgment
MFT	Meter Fix Crossing Time/Slot Time
MH	**magnetic heading**
MHA	Minimum Holding Altitude
Mhg	MegHERTZ
MHz	**megahertz**
MIA	Minimum IFR Altitudes
Mic	**microphone**
MIDO	Manufacturing Inspection District Office
MIN	**minute(s)/minimum**
MIS	Meteorological Impact Statement
MISC	Miscellaneous

MISO	Manufacturing Inspection Satellite Office
MIT	Miles In Trail
MITRE	Mitre Corporation
MLG	**main landing gear**
MLS	Microwave Landing System
MM	Middle Marker
MMC	Maintenance Monitoring Console
MMS	Maintenance Monitoring System
MNPS	Minimum Navigation Performance Specification
MNPSA	Minimum Navigation Performance Specifications Airspace
MOA	Memorandum of Agreement
MOA	Military Operations Area
MOBREP	**Mobility Representative**
MOCA	Minimum Obstruction Clearance Altitude
MOCA	**minimum obstruction clearance altitude**
MODE C	Altitude-Encoded Beacon Reply
MODE C	Altitude Reporting Mode of Secondary Radar
MODE S	Mode Select Beacon System
MOU	Memorandum of Understanding
MPO	Metropolitan Planning Organization
MPS	Maintenance Processor Subsystem (OR) Master Plan Supplement
MRA	Minimum Reception Altitude
MRC	Monthly Recurring Charge
MRK	**Marker Beacon**
MSA	Minimum Safe Altitude
MSAW	Minimum Safe Altitude Warning
MSL	Mean Sea Level
MSN	Message Switching Network
MSTR	**master**
MTC	**minimum terrain clearance**
MTCS	Modular Terminal Communications System
MTI	Moving Target Indicator
MTR	**motor**
MUX	Multiplexor
MVA	Minimum Vectoring Altitude

MVFR	Marginal Visual Flight Rules
MVOX	**microphone VOX**

N

N	**north**
N/A	**not applicable**
NAAQS	National Ambient Air Quality Standards
NACA	**National Advisory Committee for Aeronautics**
NADA	NADIN Concentrator
NADIN	National Airspace Data Interchange Network
NADSW	NADIN Switches
NAILS	National Airspace Integrated Logistics Support
NAMS	NADIN IA
NAPRS	National Airspace Performance Reporting System
NAS	National Airspace System or Naval Air Station
NASDC	National Aviation Safety Data
NASP	National Airspace System Plan
NASPAC	National Airspace System Performance Analysis Capability
NAT MNPS	**North Atlantic Minimum Navigation Performance Specification**
NATCO	National Communications Switching Center
NAV	**navigate/navigation**
NAVAID	Navigational Aid
NAVMN	Navigation Monitor and Control
NAWAU	National Aviation Weather Advisory Unit
NAWPF	National Aviation Weather Processing Facility
NB	**nondirectional beacon**
NCAR	National Center for Atmospheric Research; Boulder, CO
NCF	National Control Facility
NCIU	NEXRAD Communications Interface Unit
NCP	Noise Compatibility Program
NCS	National Communications System
NDB	**Navigation Database**
NDB	Non-Directional Radio Homing Beacon
NDB	**nondirectional beacon**
NDNB	NADIN II

NEM	Noise Exposure Map
NEPA	National Environmental Policy Act
NESA	**Non-electrostatic Shield Formula A (Windshield Anti-icing)**
NEUT	**neutral**
NEXRAD	Next Generation Weather Radar
NFAX	National Facsimile Service
NFDC	National Flight Data Center
NFIS	NAS Facilities Information System
NI	Network Interface
NICS	National Interfacility Communications System
NLG	**nose landing gear**
NM	Nautical Mile
NMAC	Near Mid Air Collision
NMC	National Meteorological Center
NMCE	Network Monitoring and Control Equipment
NMCS	Network Monitoring and Control System
NO.	**number**
NOAA	National Oceanic and Atmospheric Administration
NOC	Notice of Completion
NOPAC	**North Pacific (Airspace)**
NORM	**normal**
NOS	**National Ocean Service**
NOTAM	Notice to Airmen
NPDES	National Pollutant Discharge Elimination System
NPE	Non-primary Airport Entitlement
NPIAS	National Plan of Integrated Airport Systems
NPRM	Notice of Proposed Rulemaking
NR	Non-Rulemaking; refers to a type of airport airspace analysis case
NRA	Non-Rulemaking Airport; refers to a type of airport airspace analysis case
NRC	Non-Recurring Charge
NRCS	National Radio Communications Systems
NSAP	National Service Assurance Plan
NSRCATN	National Strategy to Reduce Congestion on America's Transportation Network

NSSFC	National Severe Storms Forecast Center
NSSL	National Severe Storms Laboratory; Norman, OK
NSWRH	NWS Regional Headquarters
NTAP	Notices To Airmen Publication
NTP	National Transportation Policy
NTS	**negative torque signal**
NTSB	National Transportation Safety Board
NTZ	No Transgression Zone
NWS	National Weather Service
NWSR	NWS Weather Excluding NXRD
NXRD	Advanced Weather Radar System
NZ	**navigation computer**

O

OAG	Official Airline Guide
OALT	Operational Acceptable Level of Traffic
OAT	**outside air temperature**
OAW	Off-airway Weather Station
OB CLR HT MSL	**obstacle clearance height mean sea level**
ODAL	Omnidirectional Approach Lighting System
ODAPS	Oceanic Display and Processing Station
OEI	One Engine Inoperative
OEP	Operational Evolution Plan / Partnership
OFA	Object Free Area
OFDPS	Offshore Flight Data Processing System
OFT	Outer Fix Time
OFZ	Obstacle Free Zone
OM	**Operating Manual**
OM	Outer Marker
OMB	Office of Management and Budget
ONER	Oceanic Navigational Error Report
OPLT	Operational Acceptable Level of Traffic
OPSCON	**Operations Control Center**
OPSW	Operational Switch
OPX	Off Premises Exchange
ORD	Operational Readiness Demonstration
OT	**other traffic**

OTR	Oceanic Transition Route
OTS	Organized Track System
OUTBD	**outbound**
OV	**other vehicle (radar)**
OVRD	**override**
OXY	**oxygen**

P

P	**Pilot**
P/S	**pitch sync**
P/S	**power section**
PA	**Public Address**
PABX	Private Automated Branch Exchange
PAD	Packet Assembler/Disassembler
PAL	Planning Activity Level
PAM	Peripheral Adapter Module
PAPI	Precision Approach Path Indicator
PAR	Precision Approach Radar
PAR	Preferential Arrival Route
PAST	**pilot-activated self-test**
PATWAS	Pilots Automatic Telephone Weather Answering Service
PBB	Passenger Boarding Bridge
PBCT	Proposed Boundary Crossing Time
PBE	**protective breathing equipment**
PBRF	Pilot Briefing
PBX	Private Branch Exchange
PCA	Positive Control Airspace
PCC	Portland Cement Concrete
PCDR	**procedure**
PCL	**pilot-controlled lighting**
PCM	Pulse Code Modulation
PDAR	Preferential Arrival And Departure Route
PDC	Pre-Departure Clearance
PDC	Program Designator Code
PDN	Public Data Network
PDR	Preferential Departure Route
PERF	**performance**

PF	**Pilot-Flying**
PFC	Passenger Facility Charge
PFD	**Primary Flight Display**
PGE	**page**
PGP	Planning Grant Program
PIC	**Pilot-in-Command**
PIC	Principal Interexchange Carrier
PIDP	Programmable Indicator Data Processor
PIF	**Personnel Information Form**
PIREP	Pilot Weather Report
PM	**Pilot-Monitoring**
PMS	Program Management System
PNR	**Point of No Return**
POI	**Principal Operations Inspector**
POL	**petroleum, oil, and lubricants**
POLIC	Police Station
POP	Point of Presence
POS	**position**
POST	**power-on system test**
POT	Point of Termination
PPH	**pounds per hour**
PPIMS	Personal Property Information Management System
PR	Primary Commercial Service Airport
PRECHK	**precheck**
PRESS	**pressure/pressurization**
PREV	**previous**
PRI	Primary Rate Interface
PRI/PRIM	**primary**
PRM	Precision Runway Monitor
PROG	**progress**
PROP	**propeller**
PROT	**Protective**
PSDN	Public Switched Data Network
Psi	**pounds per square inch**
Psig	**pounds per square inch gauge**
PSN	Packet Switched Network
PSS	Packet Switched Service
PSTN	Public Switched Telephone Network

PT	**procedure turn or proximate traffic**
PTC	Presumed-to-Conform
PTT	**push-to-talk**
PUB	Publication
PUP	Principal User Processor
PVC	Permanent Virtual Circuit
PVD	Plan View Display
PWR	**power**

Q

QA	Quality Assurance
QRH	**Quick-Reference Handbook**
QTY	**quantity**

R

R/G	**reduction gear**
RA	**Resolution Advisory**
RAIL	Runway Alignment Indicator Lights
RAIM	**Receiver Autonomous Integrity Monitor**
RAPCO	Radar Approach Control (USAF)
RAPCON	Radar Approach Control (FAA)
RATCC	Radar Air Traffic Control Center
RATCF	Radar Air Traffic Control Facility (USN)
RBC	Rotating Beam Ceilometer
RBDPE	Radar Beacon Data Processing Equipment
RBSS	Radar Bomb Scoring Squadron
RCAG	Remote Communications Air/Ground
RCC	Rescue Coordination Center
RCCC	Regional Communications Control Centers
RCF	Remote Communication Facility
RCIU	Remote Control Interface Unit
RCL	Radio Communications Link
RCL	**recall**
RCLR	RCL Repeater
RCLT	RCL Terminal
RCO	Remote Communications Outlet
RCR	**Runway Condition Reading**

RCT	**rain echo attenuation compensation technique**
RCU	Remote Control Unit
RDAT	Digitized Radar Data
RDP	Radar Data Processing
RDSIM	Runway Delay Simulation Model
RECM	**recommend**
RECT	**rectifier**
REF	**reference**
REFR	**refrigerator**
REIL	Runway End Identification Lights
REILs	**runway end identification lights**
REJ	**rejected (message)**
REL	**release**
RESYNC	**resynchronize**
REV	**reverse**
RF	**radio frequency**
RF	Radio Frequency
RFCF	**runway field clearance floor**
RGB	**engine reduction hear unit assembly**
RH	**right hand**
RL	General Aviation Reliever Airport
RMCC	Remote Monitor Control Center
RMCF	Remote Monitor Control Facility
RMI	**radio magnetic indicator**
RML	Radio Microwave Link
RMLR	RML Repeater
RMLT	RML Terminal
RMM	Remote Maintenance Monitoring
RMMS	Remote Maintenance Monitoring System
RMS	Remote Monitoring Subsystem
RMSC	Remote Monitoring Subsystem Concentrator
RMT	**remote**
RMU	**Radio Management Unit**
RNAV	Area Navigation
RNG	**range**
RNP	Required Navigation Performance
ROD	Record of Decision
RON	**remaining overnight**

ROSA	Report of Service Activity
ROT	Runway Occupancy Time
RP	Restoration Priority
RPC	Restoration Priority Code
RPG	Radar Processing Group
RPM	**revolutions per minute**
RPTG	**reporting**
RPZ	Runway Protection Zone
RRH	Remote Reading Hygrothermometer
RRHS	Remote Reading Hydrometer
RRWDS	Remote Radar Weather Display
RRWSS	RWDS Sensor Site
RSA	Runway Safety Area
RSAT	Runway Safety Action Team
RSB	**radio system bus**
RSS	Remote Speaking System
RT & BTL	Radar Tracking And Beacon Tracking Level
RT	Remote Transmitter
RTA	**recall transmitter antenna**
RTAD	Remote Tower Alphanumerics Display
RTCA	Radio Technical Commission for Aeronautics
RTP	Regional Transportation Plan
RTR	Remote Transmitter/Receiver
RTRD	Remote Tower Radar Display
RVR	Runway Visual Range
RVR	**runway visual range**
RW	Runway
RWDS	Same as RRWDS
RWP	Real-time Weather Processor

S
S	**south**
S/S	Sector Suite
SAC	Strategic Air Command
SAFI	Semi Automatic Flight Inspection
SAFO	**Safety Alert for Operators**
SALS	Short Approach Lighting System

SAT	**static air temperature**
SATCOM	Satellite Communications
SAWRS	**Supplementary Aviation Weather Reporting Station**
SAWRS	Supplementary Aviation Weather Reporting System
SB	**Service Bulletin**
SBGP	State Block Grant Program
SCC	System Command Center
SCVTS	Switched Compressed Video Telecommunications Service
SDF	Simplified Direction Finding
SDF	Software Defined Network
SDIS	Switched Digital Integrated Service
SDP	Service Delivery Point
SDS	Switched Data Service
SEC	**second/secondary**
SECT	**sector scan**
SEL	**select/selector/selected**
SEL	Single Event Level
SELF	Simplified Short Approach Lighting System With Sequenced Flashing Lights
SET	**setting**
SFAR-38	Special Federal Aviation Regulation 38
SG	**symbol generator**
SHP	**shaft horsepower**
SHPO	State Historic Preservation Officer
SIC	**Second-in-Command**
SIC	Service Initiation Charge
SID	Standard Instrument Departure
SID	Station Identifier
SIGMET	Significant Meteorological Information
SIMMOD	Airport and Airspace Simulation Model
SIP	State Implementation Plan
SKP	**skip**
SLV	**slave**
SM	Statute Miles
SMGC	Surface Movement Guidance and Control
SMP	**Service Manual Publication**

SMPS	Sector Maintenance Processor Subsystem
SMS	Safety Management System
SMS	Simulation Modeling System
SNR	Signal-to-Noise Ratio, also: S/N
SOAR	System of Airports Reporting
SOC	Service Oversight Center
SOIR	Simultaneous Operations On Intersecting Runways
SOIWR	Simultaneous Operations on Intersecting Wet Runways
SP	**Special Permit**
SPD	**speed**
SPR	**single-point refueling**
SQ	**squelch**
SRAP	Sensor Receiver and Processor
SRM	Safety Risk Management
SRN	**Short-Range Navigation**
SSALF	SSALS with Sequenced Flashers
SSALR	Simplified Short Approach Lighting System
SSB	**single side band**
SSB	Single Side Band
STA	**station**
STAB	**stabilize**
STAR	Standard Terminal Arrival Route
STBY	**standby**
STC	**Supplemental Type Certificate**
STCK	**stuck**
STD	Standard
STMUX	Statistical Data Multiplexer
STO	**store**
STOL	Short Takeoff and Landing
STS	**status**
SUPPR	**suppressor**
SURPIC	Surface Picture
SVCA	Service A
SVCB	Service B
SVCC	Service C
SVCO	Service O

SVFB	Interphone Service F (B)
SVFC	Interphone Service F (C)
SVFD	Interphone Service F (D)
SVFO	Interphone Service F (A)
SVFR	Special Visual Flight Rules
SW	**switch**
SYN	**synchronize/synchronizer**

T

T1MUX	T1 Multiplexer
TA	**Traffic Advisory**
TAAS	Terminal Advance Automation System
TAC	Technical Advisory Committee
TACAN	Tactical Aircraft Control and Navigation
TACC	**Tanker Airlift Control Center**
TACR	TACAN at VOR, TACAN only
TAD	**Terrain Alerting and Display**
TAF	Terminal Area Forecast, Terminal Aerodrome Forecast
TARS	Terminal Automated Radar Service
TAS	True Air Speed
TAS	**true airspeed**
TAT	**true air temperature**
TATCA	Terminal Air Traffic Control Automation
TAVT	Terminal Airspace Visualization Tool
TAWS	**Terrain Awareness Warning System**
TCA	Terminal Control Area
TCA	Traffic Control Airport or Tower Control Airport
TCACCIS	Transportation Coordinator Automated Command and Control Information System
TCAS	**Traffic Alert and Collision Avoidance System**
TCAS	Traffic Alert And Collision Avoidance System
TCC	DOT Transportation Computer Center
TCCC	Tower Control Computer Complex
TCE	Tone Control Equipment
TCF	**terrain clearance floor**
TCLT	Tentative Calculated Landing Time

TCO	Telecommunications Certification Officer
TCOM	Terminal Communications
TCP	**tricresyl phosphate**
TCS	Tower Communications System
TD	**temperature datum**
TDLS	Tower Data-Link Services
TDMUX	Time Division Data Multiplexer
TDPC	Touchdown/Positioning Circle
TDWR	Terminal Doppler Weather Radar
TELCO	Telephone Company
TELMS	Telecommunications Management System
TEMP	**temperature**
TERPS	Terminal Instrument Procedures
TERR	**terrain**
TFAC	To Facility
TGT	**target alert**
TH	Threshold
TH	**true heading**
TIMS	Telecommunications Information Management System
TIPS	Terminal Information Processing System
TIT	**turbine inlet temperature**
TK	**track**
TKE	**track angle error**
TL	Taxilane
TLOF	Touchdown and Liftoff Area
TM&O	Telecommunications Management and Operations
TMA	Traffic Management Advisor
TMC	Traffic Management Coordinator
TMC/MC	Traffic Management Coordinator/Military Coordinator
TMCC	Terminal Information Processing System
TMCC	Traffic Management Computer Complex
TMF	Traffic Management Facility
TML	Television Microwave Link
TMLI	Television Microwave Link Indicator
TMLR	Television Microwave Link Repeater
TMLT	Television Microwave Link Terminal

TMP	Traffic Management Processor
TMS	Traffic Management System
TMSPS	Traffic Management Specialists
TMU	Traffic Management Unit
TNAV	Terminal Navigational Aids
TO	**Technical Order**
TOC	**Top of Climb**
TOD	**Top of Descent**
TODA	Takeoff Distance Available
TOF	Time of Flight
TOFMS	Time of Flight Mass Spectrometer
TOPS	Telecommunications Ordering and Pricing System (GSA software tool)
TORA	Take-off Run Available
TR	Telecommunications Request
TR	**transformer-rectifier**
TRACAB	Terminal Radar Approach Control in Tower Cab
TRACON	Terminal Radar Approach Control Facility
TRAD	Terminal Radar Service
TRANS	**transformer/transfer/transition**
TRANSCOM	**United States Transportation Command**
TRB	Transportation Research Board
TRB	**turbulence**
TRK	**track**
TRNG	Training
TRU	**true north**
TSA	Taxiway Safety Area
TSA	**Transportation Security Administration**
TSEC	Terminal Secondary Radar Service
TSO	**technical standard order**
TSP	Telecommunications Service Priority
TSR	Telecommunications Service Request
TST	**test**
TSYS	Terminal Equipment Systems
TTMA	TRACON Traffic Management Advisor
TTY	Teletype
TVOR	Terminal VHF Omnidirectional Range

TW	Taxiway
TWEB	Transcribed Weather Broadcast
TWR	Tower (non-controlled)
TX	**transmit**
TY	Type (FAACIS)

U

UAS	Uniform Accounting System
UCI	**Unit Construction Index**
UHF	Ultra High Frequency
URA	Uniform Relocation Assistance and Real Property Acquisition Policies Act of 1970
USAF	United States Air Force
USB	**upper side band**
USC	United States Code
USOC	Uniform Service Order Code
UT	**utility**
UTC	**Universal Time Coordinated**

V

VALE	Voluntary Airport Low Emission
VASI	Visual Approach Slope Indicator
VB	**maximum turbulent air penetration speed**
VD	**maximum airspeed (dive)**
VDME	VOR with Distance Measuring Equipment
VF	Voice Frequency
VFR	Visual Flight Rules
VGSI	Visual Glideslope Indicator
VH	**maximum recommended airspeed**
VHF	Very High Frequency
VLF	Very Low Frequency
VMC	Visual Meteorological Conditions
V_{MCA}	**minimum controllable airspeed**
VNAV	**vertical navigation**
VNAV	Visual Navigational Aids
VNTSC	Volpe National Transportation System Center
VOL	**volume (audio level)**

VON	Virtual On-net
VOR	VHF Omnidirectional Range
VOR/DME	VHF Omnidirectional Range/Distance Measuring Equipment
VORTAC	VOR collocated with TACAN
VOT	VOR Test Facility
VOX	**voice**
VP/D	Vehicle/Pedestrian Deviation
V$_{REF}$	**landing reference speed**
VRS	Voice Recording System
Vs	**stall speed**
VS	**vertical speed**
VSCS	Voice Switching and Control System
VSI	**vertical speed indicator**
VSPDS	**V Speeds**
VTA	Vertex Time of Arrival
VTA	**vertical track alert**
VTAC	VOR collocated with TACAN
VTOL	Vertical Takeoff and Landing
VTS	Voice Telecommunications System

W

W	**west**
WAAS	Wide Area Augmentation System
WAN	Wide Area Network
WARN	**warning**
WC	Work Center
WCP	Weather Communications Processor
WECO	Western Electric Company
WESCOM	Western Electric Satellite Communications
WHA	Wildlife Hazard Assessment
WHMP	Wildlife Hazard Management Plan
WMSC	Weather Message Switching Center
WMSCR	Weather Message Switching Center Replacement
WOW	**weight on wheels**
WPT	**waypoint**
WRN	**warn**

WSCMO	Weather Service Contract Meteorological Observatory
WSFO	Weather Service Forecast Office
WSMO	Weather Service Meteorological Observatory
WSO	Weather Service Office
WTHR	"Weather"
WX	Weather
WX	**weather detection**

X
XSIDE	**cross-side**
XTK	**cross track**

Y
YD	**yaw damper**

Z
ZFW	**zero fuel weight**

14.0   MEASUREMENT ABBREVIATIONS

These are measurement abbreviations many of my clients use.
Depending on how often they are used in the text, I might only use them
in tables and figures, and spell out in the text; it depends on the word.
For example, I always spell out foot or feet and inch or inches in the text,
but I do define first use and then use the abbreviation for square feet or
cubic feet. This is purely based on number of characters. Since the
abbreviation for "feet" is "ft" or at some companies "ft." I don't see the
point of using "ft." throughout, which is three characters, when the actual
word is only four. Just use your best judgment.

These are measurement abbreviations many of my clients use.
Depending on how often they are used in the text, I might only use them
in tables and figures, and spell out in the text; it depends on the word.
For example, I always spell out foot or feet and inch or inches in the text,
but I do define first use and then use the abbreviation for square feet or
cubic feet. This is purely based on number of characters. Since the
abbreviation for "feet" is "ft" or at some companies "ft." I don't see the
point of using "ft." throughout, which is three characters, when the actual
word is only four. Just use your best judgment.

A

acre .... ac
acre-foot.. ac-ft
actual cubic feet per minute... acfm

alternating current... AC
ampere .... A or amp
angstrom .... Å
ante meridiem (before noon) ....a.m.
atmosphere.. atm
atomic mass unit ....amu
atomic weight ....at wt

B

barrel.. bbl
barrels per day .... bpd
below ground surface..bgs

board foot .... bd ft
boiling point ....bp
British thermal unit... Btu

C
calorie (small)..cal
calorie (large) ....Cal
centimeter...cm
centipoise...cP
cubic centimeter .... cm^3 (cc for gas volume only)
cubic centimeter-second .... cm^3-sec
cubic foot... ft^3
cubic feet per day .... cfd or ft^3/day
cubic feet per hour.. cf/h
cubic feet per minute .... cfm or ft^3/min
cubic feet per second .... cfs or ft^3/sec
cubic meter .... m^3
cubic yard ....cy
curie..Ci
cycles per minute..cpm
cycles per second.. cps or Hz

D
decibel ....dB
decibel, A-weighted..dBA
degrees Celsius..°C
degrees Fahrenheit...°F
degrees Kelvin..K
diameter...diam
direct current.. DC

E
electromagnetic force .... emf
electromagnetic unit ....emu
electron volt..eV
et alia (and others) ....et al.
et cetera ....etc.

F
foot .... ft
feet per minute.. fpm or ft/min

feet per second ....fps or ft/sec
foot-pound ....ft-lb

G

gallon ....gal
gallons per acre per day ....gpad
gallons per day .... gpd
gallons per minute .... gpm
gallons per second .... gps
grain .... gr
gram .... g
gram-square centimeter .... $g\text{-}cm^2$
gravitational constant...G

H

hertz ....Hz
horsepower .... hp
hour...hr
horizontal to vertical ....H:V

I

id est (that is) ....i.e.
inch .... in.
inside diameter...I.D.

J

joule ....J

K

kelvin (temperature unit) ....K
Kelvin (temperature scale)..K
kilo... k

kilocycles per second (kilohertz)...kHz
kilocalorie...kcal
kiloelectron volt..keV
kilogram... kg
kilometer.. km
kilovolt...kV
kilovolt ampere..kVA
kilowatt ....kW
kilowatt-hour ....kWh

L
liter L

M
magnification (power of) .... X (*e.g.*, 5X)
mean lower low water .... MLLW
mean low water .... MLW
mean sea level .... MSL
mega (million) .... M
megahertz .... MHz
megavolt .... MV
megawatt .... MW
melting point .... mp
meter .... m
metric ton .... metric ton or tonne
microgram .... µg
microgram per kilogram .... µg/kg (same as ppb)
microgram per liter .... µg/L (same as ppb)
microliter .... µL
micrometer .... µm
micromho .... µmho
micromolar .... µM or µ<u>M</u>
micromoles .... µmol
micron (micrometer) .... µm
microsiemen .... µS
mile .... mi
milliequivalent .... meq
milligram .... mg
milligram per kilogram .... mg/kg (same as ppm)
milligram per liter .... mg/L (same as ppm)
milliliter .... ml (for liquid capacity; for gases, use cc)
millimeter .... mm
millimicron .... mµ
million gallons per day .... mgd
million electron volts .... MeV
million standard cubic feet per day .... mscfd
millivolt .... mv
milliwatt .... mw
minute .... min

molar .... M or $\underline{M}$
molecular weight .... mol wt
mole percent .... mol %
month .... mo.

N
nanocurie .... nCi
normal (concentration) .... N or $\underline{N}$
normal cubic meters .... Nm^3
ounce .... oz
outside diameter .... O.D.

P
page .... p.
pages .... pp.
parts per billion .... ppb
parts per billion by volume .... ppbv
parts per million .... ppm
parts per million by volume .... ppmv
percent   .... % (*in tables, spell out in text*)
post meridiem (after noon) .... p.m.
pound .... lb
pounds per cubic foot .... pcf or lb/ft^3
pounds per square foot .... psf or lb/ft^2
pounds per square inch .... psi
pounds per square inch, absolute .... psia
pounds per square inch gauge .... psig

Q
quart .... qt

S
second .... sec or s
specific gravity .... sp gr
square centimeter .... sq cm or cm^2
square feet .... sq ft or ft^2
standard cubic feet per minute .... scfm
standard deviation .... SD
standard error of the mean .... SE

T

temperature (tables only) .... temp.

thousand (kilo) .... k

ton, metric .... metric ton or tonne

tons per day .... tpd

V

versus (tables only) .... vs.

volt V

volume per volume .... v/v

volume percent .... vol%

W

watt .... W

watt-hour .... W-hr

week .... wk

weight .... wt

weight per volume .... w/v

weight percent .... wt %

Y

yard .... yd

year .... yr

years before present .... ybp

ABOUT THE AUTHOR

Lori Jo Oswald is a freelance technical writer and technical editor who lives in Palmer, Alaska. She received her Ph.D. in English from the University of Oregon in 1994, and later earned a computer science degree. During graduate school, she began her career as a technical writer and editor, and has been writing and editing reports ever since. Additionally, she has taught English and Business Communications at Umpqua Community College, Lane Community College, and the University of Oregon, all in Oregon; Green River Community College in Washington; and the University of Alaska Anchorage. Her businesses include Wordsworth LLC, a technical editing company (wordsworthwriting.net) and Forms in Word (a document design and formatting company). She has also volunteered for humane societies for over 30 years.

Education-based Books by Lori Jo Oswald:

Children's Realistic Animal Fiction of Twentieth-Century North America

Priority on Learning: How School Districts and Schools Are Concentrating Their Scarce Resources on Academics

Quality Work Teams: Rationale and Implementation Guidelines

School-based Management: Rationale and Implementation Guidelines

Style Guide for Architectural, Engineering, Environmental, and Construction Firms

Style Guide for Oil Companies and Contractors

Made in the USA
Las Vegas, NV
07 August 2022

52894161R00125